Prince Edward County
Treasury

Town hill, Bridge Street, Picton.

Prince Edward County

TREASURY

by *Alan R. Capon*

INCLUDING

The Capt. JOHN PEPPER DOWNES
Drawings of 1847

FACSIMILE PAGES FROM THE
1865 PRINCE EDWARD DIRECTORY

ALSO A Portfolio of
Prince Edward County Aerial Photographs
by Lloyd E. Thompson

The Picton Gazette, Picton, Ontario

Also by Alan R. Capon:

His Faults Lie Gently:
the Incredible Sam Hughes

Stories of Prince Edward County

Historic Lindsay

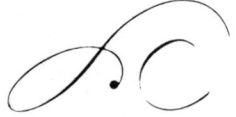

Prince Edward County Treasury: Gazette Canadiana Series
(Joseph Cembal, President; Alan R. Capon, Editor), © 1976
The Picton Gazette Publishing Co. (1971) Limited, 74a King
Street, Picton, Ontario, K0K 2T0. First Printing 1976. All
rights reserved. ISBN 0-920028-00-4

Contents

ACKNOWLEDGEMENTS

The author gratefully acknowledges the helpful co-operation of the following individuals for loaning pictures and other material used in this book:

Lloyd E. Thompson, C. W. Kettlewell, Tim Walker, Mrs. Vera Myatt, Mrs. Valerie Creasy, Mrs. Carolyn Love, Willis Metcalfe, James Gooding, Bill Thorley, Kenneth Pooley, and the Public Archives of Canada.

Hugh Macdonald, father of John A. operated a grist mill at Stone Mills (Glenora) and the announcement above was published in the Hallowell Free Press, May, 1833.

1.

You'll never die, Sir John!

Sir John A. Macdonald, Canada's first prime minister, a politician who could tell an audience "you'd rather have John A. drunk than George Brown sober" had many connections with Picton and Prince Edward County.

Many are the stories told of him during his sojourn in Picton and one was of the time when he was a law student and he and some other men found a dead horse frozen stiff on the street.

The young men thought it would be a fine joke to place the horse in the Methodist Church at the end of Chapel Street and this they did placing the animal in the pulpit, seated in the chair with its two front hooves on the reading desk.

Reportedly the old sexton had been at a meeting and came back to the church and began lighting the candles when he discovered the apparition in the pulpit. He ran from the church crying that the devil was there.

A great number of people gathered but it was some time before anyone plucked up enough courage to go in. Eventually some men went into the church with lanterns and removed the dead horse.

According to the late Gordon Walmsley, County Crown Attorney, a young man of the town was put on trial for the offence and was convicted on circumstantial evidence. The young man had not been among the crowd who had taken part in the affair and this so impressed Sir John A. Macdonald that he afterwards stated he would never allow a man to be hanged on purely circumstantial evidence.

A fight between young John A. Macdonald and a Dr. Thomas Moore brought both of them to court in October, 1834, both charged with assault.

John A. pleaded not guilty to the charge and was acquitted but Dr. Moore's case resulted in a conviction and the doctor was fined sixpence (around 12 cents at the time).

The four witnesses for the prosecution of the future first prime minister of Canada in the case were David Barker, Henry J. Bonnycastle, Benjamin Hubbs, and Francis W. Smith.

A well known story relates to the first case John A.

Sir John A. Macdonald

- Public Archives Canada C 6512

Macdonald fought in the Picton court house. John A. and the opposing counsel became involved in an argument which waxed hotter and hotter and led to blows.

The offended judge ordered the court crier to enforce order in the courtroom. The old man, a friend of John A. cried out in loud tones "Order in the Court, Order in the Court!" adding in a low and sympathetic voice as he neared the combatants, "Hit him again John!"

It was in 1830 that Macdonald, then 15 years of age, entered upon the study of law in the office of George Mackenzie of Kingston, a close friend of his father. In 1832 Mr. Mackenzie opened a branch office in Napanee and apprentice Macdonald attended there as manager. In 1833, by an arrangement made between Mr. Mackenzie and Lowther P. Macpherson, a relative of the Macdonalds, he was sent to Hallowell (Picton), to take charge of the law-office during Mr. Macpherson's absence from Canada. The 18 year old handled the office so well, that prominent citizens offered him one hundred pounds to stay.

John A. Macdonald was no stranger to Prince Edward County. His father Hugh and mother Helen operated a grist mill at Stone Mills (Glenora) after previous business ventures in Kingston and Hay Bay had failed. John was about 10 years of age when he moved to Stone Mills.

During his stay in Hallowell Macdonald became the first secretary of the Hallowell Young Men's Society, and the Prince Edward District School Board appointed him secretary. It was his first municipal office. His name can be seen at the bottom of advertisements in early issues of the Hallowell Free Press.

In 1834, many parts of Ontario were stricken by an epidemic of Asiatic cholera. One of the victims was Macdonald's former employer, George Mackenzie. John A. returned to Kingston to take over the practice.

Picton had, at one time, two newspapers, The Picton Times and The Picton Gazette, and on Friday, June 12, 1891, following the death of Canada's first prime minister the Times editor wrote: "He had lived much beyond the allotted three score and ten. He had taken advantage of and, at times had made opportunities without scruple in order to success in the line of life which he had chosen."

The editor commented on the tendency of newspapers at that time "to gush" over the late prime minister noting the injunction to not speak ill of the dead. The writer said that the career of a public man was, however public property and history had to be recorded truthfully.

The article said Macdonald was "pre-eminently a political pirate" and added "he was but little of the statesman; the longer he lived he became less entitled to high distinction in that line..."

9

PRINCE EDWARD DISTRICT
SCHOOL.

The Trustees of the Prince Edward District School, having read a letter in the Hallowell Free Press signed James Rogers, dated at Demorestville June 30th 1834, arraigning their conduct in the nomination of the Rev'd. Moses Marcus to the office of Teacher of the said District School, do hereby resolve and declare:—

That the said appointment of the Rev'd. Moses Marcus to the said office, was strictly made in accordance with the provisions of the act of Parliament relative to Public Schools:—

That the testimonials of the said Rev'd. Gentleman, were such as to satisfy the Trustees, beyond all doubt, that he was a fit, and discreet person, in morals, temper, and acquirements, to hold the said office:—

That they did not appoint him to the said office as "an alms granted through sympathy &c," nor "through the channel of private influence" nor "as a mere stranger on the *ipse dixit* of another" but solely upon the strength of his own testimonials, and with a view to the public good:—

That in this appointment, the six trustees who were present, namely, Simeon Washburn Esq. chairman; Lowther P. Macpherson Esq. Secy. Mr Sheriff Bullock; James Dougall; and David L. Fairfield, Esquires; and Doctor Moore were unanimous, and that the other trustees viz: the **Rev'd. W. Macaulay; Asa Werden;** James Cotter, and David Smith Esquires, have fully concurred in, and approved of the said appointment.

By order of the Board,
JOHN A. MACDONALD.
Secretary, Pro Tem.

Hallowell 2nd August 1834.

Announcement in Hallowell Free Press of 2nd August, 1834.

10

Sir John A. Macdonald c. 1856
- Public Archives Canada C 3813

John A. Macdonald was secretary of the Prince Edward District School Board in 1834. Advertisement from the Hallowell Free Press.

The long editorial commented on his "shameful transactions" in the Pacific scandal and said his "so-called national policy was one of the most impudent frauds ever perpetuated upon a gullible people."

"We have lightly touched upon a few of the sinister features in Sir John Macdonald's record. It is not to be inferred that we would put that record forward as one of unqualified badness."

The editor of The Picton Gazette was appalled at his contemporary at The Picton Times. In a rebuttal headed "The ghouls at work" the editor wrote: "It is the custom among savage and depraved races, that seem to be destitute of the moral sense, to sneak back to the field where some great battle has been fought and some mighty chieften had fallen, and mutilate the dead. Last Thursday, June 11th, when the earth clods were falling on the coffin of Sir John Alexander Macdonald - when sad hearts felt as if stunned by the national calamity that had befallen them - the newsboy was delivering to the subscribers of The Picton Times its last diatribe against the illustrious dead, the wail of a disappointed man."

"More in sorrow than in wrath do we deprecate the savagery that unsheaths the knife amid the shadows of the funeral chamber and violates the amenities of civilized life at the very precints of the grave."

Despite the fulminations of the Times, the spirit of Sir John A. Macdonald continued to live on in Prince Edward County to this day, and many in the area agree with the nameless supporter who cried out at one of Macdonald's political meetings, "You'll never die, Sir John!"

It was to be the verdict of history.

Picton Bay from a sketch in Picturesque Canada 1888.

2.

How Picton got its name.

If Rev. William Macaulay had not been a strong-willed man Picton might have become known as Port William or even as Adelaide or Victoria.

The name Port William was proposed at a meeting in November, 1834 after a dispute over the name of the county town reached a head, and received the largest number of votes.

Two separate villages, Hallowell Bridge and Picton had gown up each side of the Bay after pioneer settlement in this area. For a long time the names of Hallowell and Picton were used interchangeably although files of the Hallowell Free Press record the continuing controversy.

In 1834 the population of the two villages was around, 1,100 persons and it was in February, 1832 that meetings were called "for the purpose of procuring and deciding upon a plan and elevation of a Jail and Court-House, to be built at Picton," under the provisions of an Act of the Legislature passed that year.

Tenders were called on March 20, 1832 and it was built on land in Picton donated by Rev. Macaulay. He also contributed a $200 grant. The building was first used for court purposes on April 7, 1834 and John A. Macdonald made his first speech on that occasion to a jury.

The erecting of the Court House on the Picton side intensified the controversy over the name and the editor of The Free Press wrote in the August 18, 1834 edition: "We are fully convinced that the dispute between the villages of Hallowell and Picton, with respect to the name is very prejudicial to the interests of both, and we doubt not but it has been the means of deterring some persons from settling amongst us."

"A stranger coming into the District asks which is the District Town? And how shall we answer his question? Some will tell him that Picton is the district town, because within its boundaries the Court House and Jail are situated; others will set forth the claims of Hallowell to that title because its population greatly exceeds the population of Picton, until at last he perceives with surprise that we have no district Town."

PUBLIC MEETING ON WEDNES-
DAY NEXT.

Hallowell Oct. 13th 1834.

Sir.

We the undersigned request you will call a Public meeting of the inhabitants of this District to consider the propriety of petitioning the legislature for an act to unite the villages of Picton and Hallowell under another name and to define the limits of the same as a District Town.

To Richard Bullock Esquire. }
Sheriff. }

Owen Richards
D. B. Stevenson
H. W. G. Bonnycastle
Garret Striker
Alex'r. V. Allen
J. G. Sallans
A. P. Sheriff
James Wycott
Andrew Wycott
R. J. Chapman
John McCuaig
Rod. Ross
Wm. Page
John Vancount
Aaron D. Dougall
H. S. Gurney
Isaac Scott
Thomas J. Buckley
Wm. Cook
John W. Martin
Joseph Reynolds
Capt. William Clark
Moses Carnahan
Thomas Moore
Richard T. Gardiner
Tho's. Morgan
D. M. Hopkins
James Ramsay
Stewart Wilson
Shomas Nash
Benjn. Hubbs
James Dougall
Roger B. Conger
Abraham T. V. Pruyn
John Anderson
Norman Landon
Wilson Bentley

James Macdonald
Wm. Foster
Calvin Pier
Chas. Bockus
Henry Ashley
Cecil Mortimer
David Barker
Joseph Wilson
John Dougall
David Smith
James Cook
F. W. Smith
Luke Wallace
John A. Macdonald
John Jones
Joshua Hicks
Jacob Ferguson
John T. Wilson
Richard Young
J. H. Ferguson
James Scott
Richard Russell
James H. Swail
N. Ellison

Hallowell Oct. 24th 1834.

In compliance with the above requisition, I do hereby request a public meeting of the inhabitants of the District of Prince Edward, at the Court House on Wednesday the 29th inst. at the hour of two o'-clock, P. M.

RICHARD BULLOCK.
Sheriff.

This advertisement from the Hallowell Free Press, 13th October, 1834 announces the public meeting to discuss the uniting of Picton and Hallowell "under another name."

"How long shall we continue thus disunited?" asked the editor, "And how long shall jarring interests be allowed to retard the general prosperity? It is our earnest desire to see Hallowell and Picton, incorporated together under one common name, and to see the limits of the Town thus formed defined by Act of Parliament."

"By so doing, one great cause of jealousy would be removed; the inhabitants would begin to see that the interest of one part of the town was the interest of the other and as the population of the new town would exceed one thousand souls, we should be entitled to send a representative to the Provincial Parliament, the District of Prince Edward would have an additional voice in the council of the Province, and thus we should not only benefit ourselves but the district at large."

A public notice appeared in the Oct. 27, 1834 edition of The Free Press, calling for a meeting of the inhabitants of the District "to consider the propriety of petitioning the legislature for an act to unite the villages of Picton and Hallowell under another name and to define the limits of the same as a District Town.

The notice is signed by 61 citizens and is addressed, in the form of a petition, to Richard Bullock, Esquire, Sheriff. The petition's names included that of John A. Macdonald as well as many merchants of the time such as Chas. Bockus and newspaper publisher Joseph Wilson.

A notice following this in the newspaper reads: "In compliance with the above requisition I do hereby request a public meeting of the inhabitants of the District of Prince Edward, at the Court House on Wednesday the 29th inst. at the hour of two o'clock, p.m."

The Nov. 3 issue of the newspaper has a brief report on the meeting: "On the 29th ult. pursuant to notice, a meeting was held in the Court House, 'to consider the propriety of petitioning the Legislature for an act to unite the villages of Hallowell and Picton under another name, and to define the limits of the same as a District Town.' Various names were proposed, but the name of PORT WILLIAM received the largest number of votes. Although we give the persons who voted for this name, credit for being actuated by the best motives, namely, a desire to prove their loyalty to his present most gracious Majesty, by adopting his name, yet we must confess that the name does not altogether please us. It is a compound name and as such is too long for general use, a name of two syllables would have been for the best."

A long letter, signed J. A. R. appears in the Nov. 10, 1834 newspaper, and comments on "the absurdity of calling the District Town of Prince Edward by two names," and states that

Entrance to Picton Harbour, c. 1900.

a narrow bay divides it into two sections.

"The inhabitants living on the one side call the town by the name of Hallowell, while those living on the other, persist in calling it Picton. Hallowell is everywhere acknowledged as the name of the District Town, and one would naturally expect that the Courts of Law would be held in it."

The writer notes that "By a strange inconsistency however, all the paper which proceed from the Court-House are dated Picton."

He suggested that "low quarrels and petty quarrels have played a part and continues "The words Hallowell and Picton are good enough in their way, and had the name been originally designated by either, the name would not have been altogether objectionable. But after it has been once recognized as Hallowell, I do not see what right or authority an individual has to alter or change that name.

The writer said he believed that rather than continue "to indulge in needless altercation" many respectable individuals seem now to wish that both the names Hallowell and Picton be dropped and a new name adopted instead. He said he had attempted to find out what the Indian names for the area were and had found it called Nemaweketonzank (Sturgeon Cove) by the Mohawks and Tsiyodenhoewaladi (Head of the Bay) by the Mississaguas. "No European tongue could learn to articulate these names under six weeks hard study," he commented.

He suggested the name Victoria might well be adopted for the Princess "who is now presumptive heiress to the throne of Great Britain."

In 1837, Picton was incorporated as a police village. At that time Abraham Barker sat on the Board of Police Commissioners. About 1847, Picton was booming and application was made to the Legislature to have Picton incorporated as a town and incorporation took place in 1850 and a mayor and council was elected. A duty of the mayor at that time was holding Mayor's Court, this was later succeeded by a magistrate's court.

When the bill to incorporate the twin villages of Hallowell and Picton was presented to the Provincial Parliament the name of Picton, Macaulay's choice was on the application. General Sir Thomas Picton, was second in command to Wellington at Waterloo, where he was killed in 1815. His mortal remains lie in St. Paul's Cathedral, London, England. General Picton was apparently either a friend or relative of the Macaulay family.

Today the name of Hallowell remains as the name of the township that surrounds the town of Picton.

Sir Sam Hughes visited Picton

3.

Hughes was foe of booze.

One of the projects of Sir Sam Hughes, the Minister of Militia and Defence in Sir Robert Borden's cabinet in the years before the first world war was to build a vast network of armouries and drill halls across the country, and these were to serve Canada well in the war that was to come in 1914.

One of the biggest and best of the many constructed was the one he built in Lindsay, Ontario, his home town (Hughes believed in political patronage), and the Town of Picton also received a handsome building which was opened in June, 1914.

The armoury building program consumed a great deal of money and stoked an enormous amount of criticism, particularly from those who, unlike Hughes, could not see war was coming.

Col. Sam, (this was before the eccentric minister had persuaded Prime Minister Borden to elevate him to Major-General, and before he was knighted by King George V,) always liked a parade, and at the opening of each armoury a parade and grand ceremonial opening was held.

The veteran politician, Sir Mackenzie Bowell came over from Belleville for the occasion. Sir Mackenzie said that 59 years earlier he had first taken the political platform in Prince Edward County. "Ninety years old, but keen in the discussion of political issues, the aged Senator is a wonder", stated a contemporary newspaper report.

Col. Hughes justified his armoury expenditures on the grounds of providing "a house of entertainment" or a "home for culture and refinement" for the boys and girls of the communities in which the armouries were located. A newspaper report of the day stated: "He took great credit to himself for abolishing the camp canteen and preventing liquor from being used on the grounds. He claimed it would be unwise to abolish the bars. Such institutions had a tendency to make the boys self-reliant. He had rigidly refrained from using intoxicating liquors himself. Presumably self-reliance is not required in the Colonel's soldier boys", commented the writer.

Hughes had always been a tee-totaller and a foe of booze and

The Armoury Picton when it was occupied by The Hastings and Prince Edward Regiment.

at one militia camp held at Niagara-on-the-Lake the militiamen had made up the following refrain:

D'ye ken Sam Hughes, he's the foe of booze,
He's the real champeen, of the dry canteen,
For the camp is dead, and we're sent to bed,
So we won't have a head in the morning.

It was to be only a month later that The Picton Gazette was to report "England Declares War Against Germany." The report stated "The greatest war of the century is now on, and it has come with a suddeness that is startling even to those who were convinced that a conflict was sooner or later inevitable."

Col. Milton K. Adams, Commanding Officer of the 155th Battalion had written to Col. Hughes the previous week, offering to enlist if his services were needed, and a few days later sent a telegram reading: "Col. Sam Hughes, Ottawa. My letter of last week tendering my services, also includes the services of the regiment under my command. In case of need give us a chance. M. Adams, Colonel."

Sam Hughes felt that the armouries that were to be built should be substantial buildings that would benefit the communities in which they were built, and provide, as well as a place for militia training, a public edifice that would serve for other community purposes.

This armoury building program alone was one that should have earned the impetuous, colourful Sam Hughes the lasting gratitude of the Canadian people, yet it was but one of his monumental achievements that have been overshadowed by his many weaknesses and peculiarities. Historians have never given Hughes the credit he so richly deserved.

Hughes was responsible for despatching overseas the first Canadian contingent from Valcartier within a few short weeks from the outbreak of war. Many men from Prince Edward County were among those who sailed for England in the great armada from Gaspe Bay, and who saw Hughes fussing among the ships in a tug distributing bundles of his 900-word valedictory "Where Duty Leads" to the soldiers.

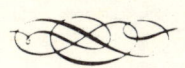

Main St. Wellington, Ont.

Main Street, Wellington.

4.

Passenger Pigeon joined the dodo

So abundant were the passenger pigeons at one time in Prince Edward County and in many other parts of Ontario in the middle 1800's, that boys could stand on house tops and knock birds down with sticks as they flew over.

The wild pigeons were a source of food for the early settlers and they were slaughtered in immense numbers, and in 1914 when the last passenger pigeon toppled from its perch in a United States zoo, the bird became extinct.

The passenger pigeon visited Canada in the early spring months and in August in immense flocks, and Samuel Strickland wrote in his book "Twenty-seven years in Canada West" (1853) the following: "...in some parts of the province, early in Spring and directly after wheat harvest, their numbers are incredible. Some days they commence flying as soon as it is light in the morning, and continue, flock after flock, until sun-down. To calculate the sum total of birds passing even on one day, appears to be impossible. I think, the greatest masses fly near the shore of the great Canadian lakes, and sometimes so low that they may be easily killed with a horse-pistol, or even knocked down with a long pole."

Joseph Pickering wrote in "Inquiries of an Emigrant" (1831): "Pigeons, in great flocks, going out daily northward, some people with nets and decoy pigeons, will catch several hundred in a day, when they sometimes take only their breasts, and salt in barrels, and make beds of their feathers..."

John James Audubon, the naturalist related that in the autumn of 1813 he left his house on the banks of the Ohio to go to Louisville and he observed pigeons flying in great numbers from the north-east to the south-west. After they had been passing for an hour he dismounted and proceeded to make a dot with a pencil on paper for every flock that passed. He found in a short time that he was putting down dots at the rate of 163 in 21 minutes.

Audubon resumed his journey but still the pigeons came, the light of day darkened as if by a solar eclipse. For 55 miles Audubon travelled along with the pigeons flying overhead, the flight continuing for three days. He estimated the birds flew past in columns of about one mile wide and calculated the speed of flight at about 60 miles per hour. The birds, of course, consumed great quantities of grain.

Glenora Hill, near Picton, c.1900.

One of the last great kills recorded was in 1878 when three hundred tons of dressed birds were shipped by hunters in Michigan. By the year 1899 the great flights of the passenger pigeon were over and only the odd pair could be found breeding in the province of Ontario, except for an area in the north-west where quite a few could still be found.

Fifteen years later the passenger pigeon has joined the dodo - just a name in record books with a few stuffed birds left in museum cases.

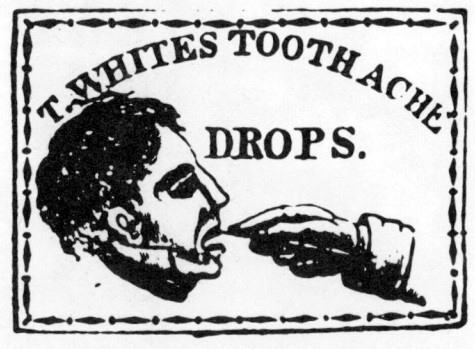

This toothache drop label is reproduced from a scrapbook kept by Sara Baker of Picton in the 1830's, now preserved in Prince Edward County Museum.

LADIES' ACADEMY

MRS. YOUMANS

INTENDS opening on the 1st of November, School for young Ladies in the building formerly occupied by C. S. Patterson, Esq., Picton, for instruction in Common and higher English, French, Music and the various departments of Painting and Drawing.

MRS. LANCE, an experienced Artist, will have charge of the Ornamental Department. Lessons in Music given by an efficient instructor.

Charges per term of eleven weeks:

Common and higher English,..........
French,................................
Needle Work,..........................
Music.................................
Drawing...............................
Water Colors,.........................
Crayon................................
Velvet Painting,......................
Oil   "   ....
Wax, Fruit and Flowers,...............
Tissue Flowers,.......................

☞ One Dollar per term extra for practice on Piano. ☜

Picton, October 4, 1858.

CAMPAIGN
ECHOES

MRS. YOUMANS

Mrs. Letitia Youmans
taught at the
Picton Ladies' Academy

5.

Echoes of a temperance campaign.

"My advice to young people, if you wish to enjoy your life and be a source of comfort to yourself and friends, **be a total** Abstainer".

This advice, hand-written on the title page of a copy of "Campaign Echoes", the autobiography of Mrs. Letitia Youmans, in the special books collection of Picton Public Library, was written by Stephen B. Conger of St. Paul, Minn., U.S.A. He wrote: "I joined Mrs. Youman's Band of Hope when she held meetings in the Conger Hall located on the corner of Bowery and Main Streets, Picton, Ontario. As a boy I walked from School house No. 4, Hallowell, a distance of three and a half miles to attend these meetings, sometimes through rain and snow storms...I have always been thankful for having joined the Band of Hope".

Mrs. Youmans was a temperance pioneer in the days when demon rum was demoralizing society and Picton alone had "nine places of legalized temptation".

An Ontario Historic Sites plaque was unveiled June 18, 1974 to her memory near her grave at Glenwood Cemetery, Picton. The text reads:

"Letitia Youmans 1827-1896. Born near Cobourg of Methodist parents, Letitia Youmans, nee Creighton, was educated at local schools and at Burlington Ladies' Academy. In 1849 she moved to Picton and taught briefly at a girls' school. Deeply religious and believing that a well-ordered Christian family was fundamental to a propserous, moral society, she viewed with alarm the threat presented to this ideal by intemperance. She became active in temperance reform and in 1874 formed a "Women's Christian Temperance Union" in Picton. Quickly becoming a leader in women's agitation for prohibitory legislation, she travelled extensively, organizing "unions" throughout Canada. Letitia Youmans was the first president of the W.C.T.U. of Ontario, (1877-82) and of the Dominion organization (1883-89). She died at Toronto and was buried in this cemetery."

Letitia was born at Baltimore, a small village near Cobourg

LETITIA YOUMANS 1827-1896

Born near Cobourg of Methodist parents, Letitia Youmans, née Creighton, was educated at local schools and at Burlington Ladies Academy. In 1849 she moved to Picton and taught briefly at a girls' school. Deeply religious and believing that a well-ordered Christian family was fundamental to a prosperous, moral society, she viewed with alarm the threat presented to this ideal by intemperance. She became active in temperance reform and in 1874 formed a "Woman's Christian Temperance Union" in Picton. Quickly becoming a leader in women's agitation for prohibitory legislation, she travelled extensively, organizing "unions" throughout Canada. Letitia Youmans was the first president of the W.C.T.U. of Ontario (1877-82) and of the Dominion organization (1883-89). She died at Toronto and was buried in this cemetery.

Erected by the Archaeological and Historic Sites Board,
Ministry of Colleges and Universities

Letitia Youmans
1827-1896

on January 3, 1827. Her father, John Creighton and her mother, Anne Bishop were both Methodists.

She was educated at local primary schools, Cobourg Ladies' Seminary and Burlington Ladies' Academy. After graduating in 1846 she taught at the latter school for two years before accepting a position at Picton Ladies' Academy.

At Picton she met and married Arthur Youmans, a prosperous miller and farmer who had eight children from a previous marriage. After the children had grown she decided to devote herself to eradicating intemperance as well as the use of tobacco and of "bad words".

When only ten she had pledged herself to a life of total abstinence and she viewed with horror the "nine places of legalized temptation" in Picton.

She placed the blame for drunkenness squarely on the heads of the liquor merchants whose activities she condemned as the "crime of crimes".

Her early reform attempts were local but in 1874 she attended a meeting at Lake Chautauqua, New York, to discuss methods of Sunday School instruction and at one of the temperance sessions held there the first steps to the formation of a Women's National Temperance Association were taken.

Full of enthusiasm, within three months Mrs. Youmans had formed a Women's Temperance Union at Picton. Just a few months earlier the first "union" in Canada had been formed at Owen Sound by Mrs. R. J. Doyle.

The Union first attempted to have the Town of Picton pass a by-law to prohibit the sale of liquor within the town limits. The municipality could take this action under the provisions of the Dunkin Bill of 1864 which allowed a probibitory by-law to be passed. The Union was unsuccessful but achieved success with Prince Edward County Council.

She was a tireless speaker and addressed audiences as many as five or six times a week. She claimed women had three inalienable rights: "the right of every women to have a comfortable home; of every wife to have a sober husband; of every mother to have sober sons."

Mrs. Youmans served five successive terms as president of the provincial Women's Christian Temperance Union and was Field Organizer for five years. Her book "Campaign Echoes", written by request of the Provincial organization, was published in 1893.

In 1888 she was stricken with inflammatory rheumatism and for the remainder of her life was a helpless invalid. She died in 1896 and was buried in Glenwood Cemetery, Picton.

Picton's Main Street in 1910.

Post Office, Picton.

Public Library, Picton, Ont.

The Public Library, Picton.

34

A parade in Picton June 12th, 1907 honouring Rodmond P. Roblin, Premier of Manitoba. He was knighted in 1912.

Dayton Murphy, Equilibrist, of Wellington

6.

Dayton Murphy, Equilibrist.

The late Dayton Murphy, Equilibrist, of Wellington, Ontario always wanted to go over Niagara Falls on a bicycle, but his mother would not let him, according to his widow Lilla Murphy.

Mrs. Murphy never saw her husband do any of his famous balancing acts because he retired from that profession just before the two were married 1905.

Photographs of his sensational bicycle and balancing feats show the variety of acts he offered during his career as an equilibrist.

A clipping in an old scrapbook from a Picton newspaper reads: "Dayton pulled off wonderful stunts on the wheel. With a gun over his shoulder he could break glass balls tossed in the air behind him while riding full speed ahead. Many daring feats were cleverly performed."

Mr. Murphy's hair raising high wire stunts were practiced on his own practice area near his house in Wellington.

He performed in Canada and the United States and used to appear in Wellington at the Dominion Day celebrations.

He had several cycles including a penny-farthing (the model with a very large front wheel and small rear wheel) as well as many other props from balancing poles to bottles.

He was a skilled marksman and would balance on his bicycle backwards and fire at a target with the aid of a mirror.

After retirement he worked for a Picton photographer and also set up a feeding area for wild geese near his home. He banded the geese and hoped to set up a bird sanctuary at West Lake.

Dayton Murphy, equilibrist, died in January, 1965 at the age of 86.

The Loyal True Blue Orphanage, opened 1898, and moved to Richmond Hill in 1923.

The annual outing of orphanage children.

Picton Business College now the location of the W. H. Williamson Insurance Co.

Public School, Picton, Ont., Canada

The Mary Street Public School, now demolished.

Mary Street, Picton.

Point Traverse fish dinner, 1896.

Cressy Cheese Factory, North Marysburgh built 1872

44

Stone Mills (Glenora) Stage and Ferry Hotel.

The West Lake Brick and Products Company.

7.

Bricks were made at Sandbanks.

Citizens of Prince Edward County heard officially in 1914 through newspaper advertisements of the intention of utilizing a part of the "picturesque and valuable" Sandbanks to make house bricks.

The advertisement, signed by L. V. Stevens announced that the writer made his first visit to the county a few months earlier and had been "amazed commercially by the reckless waste of one of the greatest assets that the county contains, the picturesque and valuable sand banks."

"Although assured by all that they possessed no value, he had a conviction that their intrinsic worth was something immense and immediately proceeded to investigate ... some persistent doubters have followed him, even gone so far as to write their doubts to his home and he has respected and thanked them, for he loves an honest doubter."

Later in the year, a Prospectus of the Westlake Brick and Products Co., Limited was issued and filed with the Provincial Secretary, September 14, 1914. The prospectus stated the authorized capital of the West Lake plant would be $250,000 and that the head office of the company would be at Fort Erie and the factory and works at the Sand Banks, West Lake, Ontario. Purpose of the company was stated as the manufacture, sale and export of brick, lime and all other articles that can be manufactured of sand, lime or both.

The incorporators and provisional directors of the company were given as Norbert Hoffman, Buffalo, N.Y., Anna Catherine Patterson, Welland, Ontario, Hugh Alexander Rose, Senior, Welland, Ontario, Hugh Alexander Rose, Junior, Welland. The company was to take over all options and property held by L. V. Stevens in and about West Lake, Ontario.

The prospectus contains a comprehensive description of the value of sand lime brick, noting that the scarcity of lumber for building purposes was well known. "At one time it was thought that the supply was inexhaustible and no more care or consideration was given to grades which we no longer see, than was given to the cheapest pine or white wood."

The company suggested brick was the most logical material for building and claimed silica or sand lime brick was low in cost and superior in use.

The Picton Times of April 2, 1914 stated: "Mr. Stevens of Buffalo, one of the gentlemen composing the West Lake Brick

Company, asked that a test be made as to the strength and durability of the Sandbanks' bricks. The following test was made in Wellington.

"A brick was soaked for ten hours in water, then taken out and allowed to freeze, after which it was thrown into a furnace and became red hot. Then it was taken out and at once thrown into a pail of water. Surely the test was a severe one. The tested brick can be seen today at the post office in a sound condition."

The British Whig of Kingston in the issue dated July 28, 1914 reported: "Wellington is all excited over new harbour and manufacture of new brick." The report of the test concludes: "The brick came through without a crack or scratch of any kind."

The prospectus noted the chief commodity in the manufacture of brick is sand and claimed the three and a half miles of sandbanks made available to the company by Government concession, with an area of 502 acres, and the private property owned by the company by purchase and option, contained a table land about three quarters of a mile in width and over one mile in length, probably 40 feet. "We are informed that outside the large deposits of Japan, ours are the largest sand hills in the world."

The author of the prospectus claimed the location was favourable because of the easy access to markets, noting that from the company's dock on West Lake that extended immediately in front of the factory, "in less than one hour's time, our boat is out of our harbour upon the waters of the Great Lakes, accessible to territory occupied by over ten million people."

It was noted: "Railroads can never compete with an old scow and a tug, and our bricks are not sensitive as to the mode of their transportation."

The writer stated that the water within 20 feet of the shore was 12 feet deep, "and there is a natural turning basin sufficiently large for any of the Great Lakes boats. And further, we are completely sheltered from the wildest storms upon the larger lakes by our vast sand hills rising to great heights within a few rods to our left. While a tempest raging upon Lake Otario, our loading goes peacefully on."

The prospectus contains estimated cost per thousand for the bricks as follows:

1 Foreman (machinist) per week	$35.00
1 Assistant Foreman (machinist)	$18.00
1 Engineer, Fireman	$18.00
1 Engineer, Night	$15.00
3 Sand Loaders	$36.00
8 men at wet pans	$80.00
8 men at presses	$20.00
4 men unloading brick	$48.00
2 Roustabouts	$20.00
1 Time Keeper and Shipping Clerk	$15.00
5 Extra (3 at $10.00, 2 at $12.00)	$54.00
Total Weekly payroll	$459.00

Drawing Brick from West Lake Brick Plant, Oct. 1922.

The estimate states that 88,000 bricks should be made each day for 528,000 brick per week with an allowance of 28,000 for seconds. Costs were calculated at $459 for labour, $160 for coal (40 tons of coal at $4.00), $270 for lime (90 tons of lime at $3.00) and $100 for wear and tear on machinery. The total cost of 500,000 bricks was calculated at $989.00 and the total cost per 1,000 bricks at $2.00.

In November, 1913 a story in The Picton Gazette reported on three men visiting Picton - L. V. Stevens, of Buffalo; J. V. Cole, Owen Sound, and Anton Berg, president of the Berg Machinery Company, Toronto bringing with them samples of brick made with sand taken "from the wonderful sand dunes of Prince Edward County." The story stated that the men hoped to erect a plant at West Lake worth half a million dollars, with a capacity of 500,000 bricks a day and then, estimated cost at less than $4 per thousand.

The brick plant was built and many houses in Prince Edward County still exist that were built of West Lake bricks. What was to bring the company to an end, however, was the inexorable movement of the sand dunes. The peninsula is oriented in such a way that it lies broadside to the full sweep of the west wind as it blows without interruption across Lake Ontario and over the years the sand drifted. Farmers had felled the virgin cedars in the area and cleared land and this aided the movement of the sand hills, the shores of West Lake were filled in, grassy flats and hollows disappeared, farm land was encroached upon, sections of the original land were blocked with sand and buildings were threatened.

One landowner moved his buildings from the old road to the new, one house was abandoned and The Evergreen Hotel was pulled down before it was buried and lost in the encroaching sand. Attempts were made to stem the tide of the sand by planting trees and by building barriers of fences of plank and lath woven on wireware to hold the sand until the trees took root. Brush and spoiled hay was also used to slow the movement of the sands.

The attempts at controlling the sand commenced in 1911 and continued for many years, nevertheless, more agricultural land was spoiled and the sand dunes built up against the back of the West Lake Brick and Products Company, eventually forcing it to close.

Today, the foundations of the brick plant can be traced in the shifting sands of the famous Prince Edward County sandbanks.

The Capt. John Pepper Downes

Drawings of 1847

- Village of Wellington.
- Main Street, Picton.
- Bay of Quinte, from Picton.
- Bryce Wharf, Picton.
- Picton Bay from Hill Street.
- Residence of Capt. J. P. Downes, Bay Shor
- Distant view from Picton.
- Residence of Ph. Low in 1847.
- English Church, Picton.
- Roman Catholic Church.

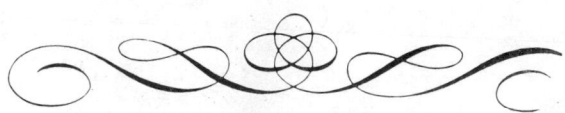

The ten illustrations reproduced in the following portfolio are from original pencil sketches made by Capt. John Pepper Downes of Picton in 1847. Capt. Downes died in his 77th year in 1878. The original sketches belong to Prince Edward County. Downes was a Captain 3rd Batt. In. Militia.

Village of Wellington.

Main Street, Picton.

53

Bay of Quinte, from Picton.

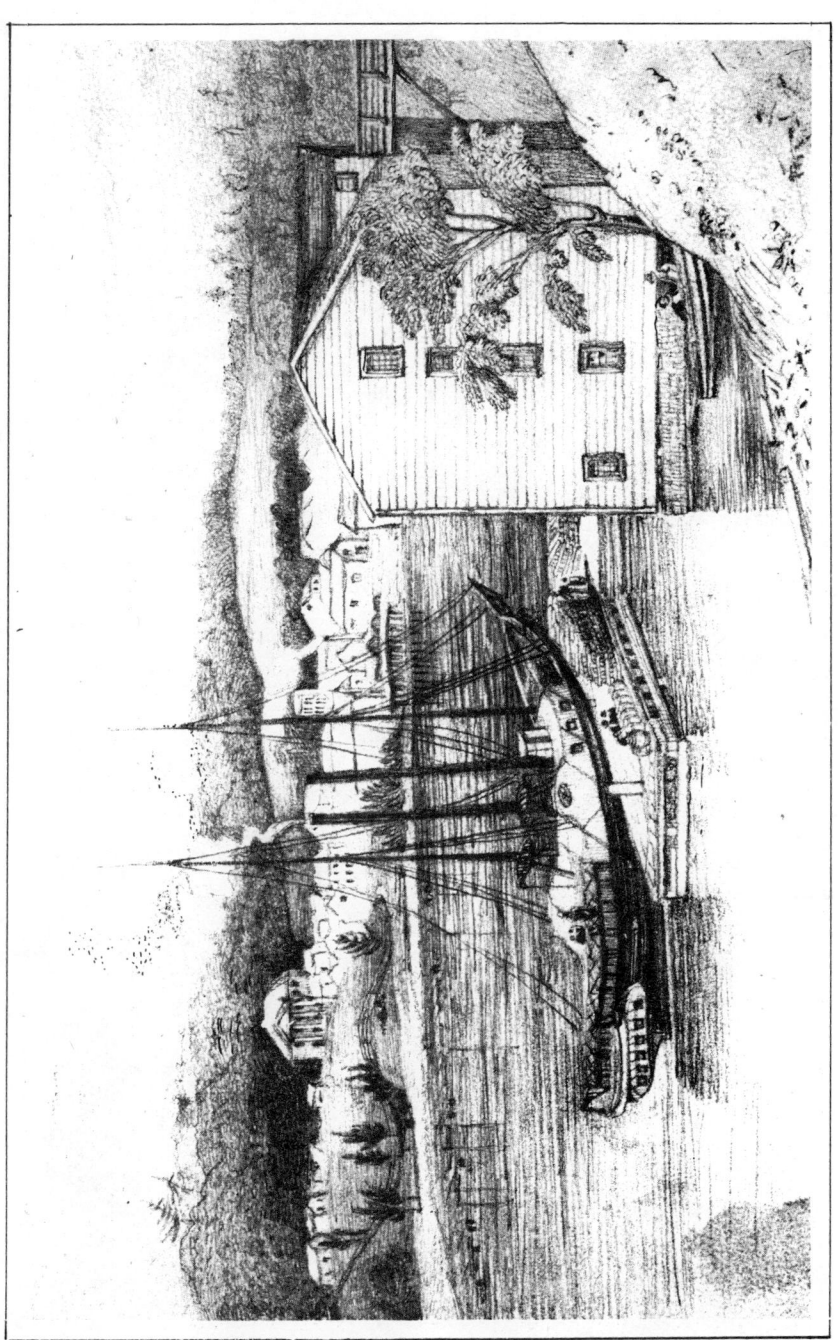

Bryce Wharf, Picton.

Picton Bay from Hill Street

Residence of Capt. J. P. Downes, Bay Shore.

Distant view from Picton.

Residence of Ph. Low in 1847.

Roman Catholic Church.

FACSIMILE PAGES

1865

PRINCE EDWARD DIRECTORY

PRINCE EDWARD

DIRECTORY

HENRY BROCK

PUBLISHER

Bay of Quinte, from above Stone Mills (Glenora) from Picturesque Canada.

Prince Edward
Directory

Selected pages from the first Directory of the Town of Picton and the County of Prince Edward, published in December, 1865 by Henry Brock are reproduced here. The directory also contained lists of the subscribers to the directory and short descriptions of the villages, as follows:

DEMORESTVILLE: "Formerly known as Sodom, is situated in the township of Sophiasburgh on the Big Marsh, and opposite the Big Island in the Bay of Quinte, was at one time a place of considerable trade, which has greatly declined the last fifteen years, owing to its proximity to the towns of Picton and Belleville.

"A long stone bridge near here, connects the Big Island with the County. It has the peculiarity of being the only bridge which the County has been called upon to expend any amount of money in building.

"The village contains a few stores, taverns, carriage and blacksmith's shops. Daily mail during winter to and from Picton and Belleville. Population, about 250."

NORTHPORT: "Is situated in the Township of Sophiasburgh, on the Bay of Quinte, four miles east of Demorestville, and fifteen from Picton. It has a church, school, and several taverns, stores, &c. Mail tri-weekly. Population, about 100."

ROBLIN'S MILLS: "Is at the head of Consecon Lake, in the Township of Ameliasburg. It has an extensive flouring mill, the property of Owen Roblin, from which it derives its name. There are a few stores, a blacksmith's shop, post office, &c., here. Mail semi-weekly. Population, about 100."

REDNERSVILLE: "Is situated in the Township of Ameliasburgh, on the Bay of Quinte, distant from Belleville three miles, has a post office, store, blacksmith's shop, tavern, &c. Population, about 50. Mail three times a week."

CONSECON: "Lies partly in the Township of Hillier, and partly in Ameliasburgh, being divided by a creek of the same name, which empties the waters of Lake Consecon into Weller's Bay, in which harbour the largest lake vessels can safely ride anchor during the most severe storms, being protected from the roughness of the lake by an extensive sand bank.

"The Government has decided, we believe, upon enlarging the mouth and dredging the harbour, which, when done, will add to the trade of the village by inducing many vessels to take advantage of its superior accommodations, and winter there.

"The village contains three stores, two blacksmiths and two carriage shops, four shoemakers, two doctors, &c.

"Mail daily to and from Brighton and Picton per Patterson's Royal Mail stage line. Population, about 350."

VILLAGE OF MILFORD: "Is situated on Black Creek, in the Township of Marysburgh, two and a half miles from Prince Edward or South Bay, where is located customs port of the same name. A considerable amount of the trade done here is derived from the vessels wintering over in the bay. It has excellent water privileges, and contains two grist mills, a post office, two stores and three taverns. Nearly every trade is here represented. Mail from Picton twice a week. Church of England service every Sunday, Methodist do. Population, about 250."

CHERRY VALLEY: "This village is well named, being situated in a beautiful valley at the head of East Lake, in the Township of Athol, five miles from Picton. It contains several churches, stores, carriage, paint, and blacksmith shops. Church of England service every second Sunday. Mail tri-weekly. Population, about 150."

WELLINGTON: "This is an incorporated village, situated partly in the Township of Hillier, the balance in Hallowell, and lying on Lake Ontario.

"The village is principally built on one long street, about one and a half miles in length, running parallel with the lake.

"It contains several stores, carriage shops, blacksmith shops, &c. Mail daily to Picton and Brighton.

"It stands next to Picton as regards trade and population, though, owing to the partial failure of the fine fishery on which its prosperity in a great measure depends, the mercantile and manufacturing interests of the place are only partly represented in our advertising columns. The Episcopal Methodists have a fine brick church built on the Main street. Having an extensive farming country on three sides and a good fishery south of it, the future prosperity and growth of the place will depend in a great measure on the energy displayed by the inhabitants in improving and profiting by these natural advantages. There is, certainly, a good opening here for practical men with moderate capital. Population, about 800."

We have included a selection of the advertisements from this Directory of over 160 pages.

The original was loaned for reproduction purposes by Mrs. Vera Myatt of Picton.

PREFACE

In presenting this, the first Directory of the Town of Picton and County of Prince Edward, to its numerous subscribers, I have to acknowledge the uniform courtesy shown to myself and agents in collecting matter for the same, and thank the merchants and manufacturers for their liberal advertisements, which I hope will prove as remunerative to them as the work will prove useful to the thousands of readers whose interest or pleasure may lead them to consult its pages. To the latter I have only to say that advertisements were only received from the leading business men, so that the pages of this work are not only a guide to the merchant but also to the purchaser; the whole work having been corrected from proof sheets, which were sent throughout the County for corection. The general public may rest assured that neither pains nor expense have been spared to make it all that could be desired even by professed fault-finders.

To those whose names have been unwittingly omitted I only have to say that all the amends that it is possible to make will be done in the next edition.

HENRY BROCK.

Montreal, December, 1865.

THE PICTON TIMES,

A REFORM JOURNAL,

Devoted to Politics, Literature, Temperance and General News,

IS PUBLISHED

EVERY TUESDAY MORNING,

IN THE TIMES BUILDING,

MAIN STREET:

Directly opposite the Wesleyan Methodist Church,

AT ONE DOLLAR PER ANNUM.

ROBERT BOYLE, Publisher and Proprietor.

The Office is well supplied with PLAIN and FANCY JOB TYPE, and the Proprietor is at all times prepared to do work with which he may be favored

Neatly, Expeditiously, and Cheaply.

COUNTY OF PRINCE EDWARD.

WHEN the thirteen American Colonies forcibly severed themselves (with the assistance of England's ancient rival and enemy) from the protection of the mother country, a large number of the colonists would not allow the illjudged legislation of a political party, who for a time held the reins of power at home, or the still more wicked, insane and ungenerous conduct of their unthinking fellow-subjects in America, to deprive them of their proud birthright as British subjects, and of the benefit to themselves and posterity of that excellent constitution and those just laws, which in their minds were associated with and hallowed by every sentiment that tends to the elevation and advancement of humanity. Preferring to live under the old flag in a strange and comparatively unexplored country, than to remain in their old homes, where the great mass of the people had thrown off allegiance to the British Crown, they came to Canada, bringing with them those high principles of loyalty and honor which their descendants yet retain, many of whom still live on the same property in Prince Edward County which was bestowed by a grateful Sovereign in appreciation of their unwavering loyalty.

The County is one of the forty-two which, combined, constitute Canada West. It contains six Townships, namely, Ameliasburg at its extreme western part, which connects it at the carrying place with the Township of Murray, County of Northumberland; Hillier, lying south of Ameliasburg on the Lake side; Sophiasburg, which includes Big Island, lying on the Bay side; Hallowell, which is south of Sophiasburg, east of Hillier, and running from the Bay to the Lake; Marysburgh, east of Hallowell, composing the extreme eastern portion of the county; Athol, south of Hallowell and Marysburgh, the smallest and most southern Township in the County.

According to the census returns of 1861, Prince Edward contained 20,869 inhabitants. It now contains probably 24,000.

It is fifty-five miles in length by about fifteen in breadth ; bounded on the north and east by the beautiful Bay of Quinte, on the south and west by Lake Ontario, which contributes to the wealth of the county by means of its valuable supply of fish, quantities of which are annually caught (particularly on the far-famed Wellington beach) and disposed of at renumerative prices in the Kingston, Montreal, and American Markets.

The County has fine harbour accommodations ; the largest are Consecon, Picton, Wellington, and Prince Edward or South Bay. The last is truly a harbour of refuge ; in it all Lake craft can ride at anchor in perfect security from the effects of the most violent storms. Point Traverse, or, as it is sometimes called, Long Point, breaks Ontario's rage, and vessels once rounding it are then perfectly safe.

The County exports immense numbers of horses, cattle, and sheep, which command the highest prices, and are eagerly sought for on account of their superior condition and breed.

The County and Township municipalities are entirely free from debt. This is owing, in a great measure, to the geographical position of the County, which is almost an island, being only connected with the main land by a neck at its north-western extremity, of about three-quarters of a mile in width. On account of its peculiar position the railway maniacs could not get sufficient local support to establish a road in opposition to the lake trade. The roads are in great part natural turnpikes, requiring little or no outlay. There are consequently no tolls collected.

As an agricultural County, Prince Edward stands high, which, with its extraordinary facilities for transportation and other important advantages, presents to the capitalist desirous of establishing manufactories, the most favorable inducements.

As regards oil, there are three lots in the County whose occupants are sanguine of becoming oil princes at some future day.

The high tone of morality which characterizes the By-laws of the County, and the strict manner in which they are enforced, may fairly stand as an index to the good habits and principles of the inhabitants generally. Other counties would do well to follow their example in this respect.

The inhabitants of the County, though they have literally covered it with good, substantial, and well-conducted schools, are still determined not to stop there, but are engaged in the laudable competition of outvieing each other with liberal individual contributions, as a subsidy to induce the Church of England to establish a college in Picton, to be called the Ontario College, conducted under the auspices of the Established Church, but free from sectarianism, and open to all denominations. A large number of the citizens of Montreal have agreed to make up any deficit that may exist after the county subscriptions have reached a certain figure. All will unite in wishing this laudable enterprise every success.

On account of the County standing as it does out in the lake, considerably beyond the rest of the shore, and being insufficiently provided with light-houses, vessels, more or less, are wrecked here every fall. This last has been a peculiarly unfortunate one, as I regret to say that not only has a large amount of property been damaged, but valuable lives have been lost. Cannot a life-boat association be formed, organized on the principle of those in Great Britain.

A medical practitioner of high standing in his profession (Dr. H. B. Evans), has noticed, and is desirous of turning to advantage, a praiseworthy characteristic which is peculiarly marked in the domestic life of the people of this County, viz., their habit of adopting as members of the family, children, and boys and girls whose parents have been removed by death, leaving them destitute of the means of support. The position of these children is thus raised above that of the menial. They are, by means of a good English education, placed in a position to become useful and respected members of society. The Doctor has published in a circular, a letter addressed by him to Thomas D'Arcy McGee, Minister of Agriculture and Emigration, and sent a copy to the different County Councils, requesting them to give the subject their consideration, and if it meets with their approval, to pass a resolution to that effect, and send a copy of the same to him for future action. The scheme is simple, practical, and self-sustaining, and will, if acted upon in a proper manner, and not abused, supply the agricultural community with a steady and reliable, because interested class of co-operatives, the want of which is felt more and more every year in developing the great productive resources of the country.

———

Following will be found a large amount of statistical information compiled from the census returns of 1861.

RETURN OF AGRICULTURAL PRODUCE FOR 1861,
COUNTY OF PRINCE EDWARD.

TOWNSHIPS, &c.	Total No. of acres.	10 acres and under.	10 to 20.	25 to 50.	50 to 100.	100 to 200.	Upwards of 200.	Amount held in acres.	Under cultivation.	Under crops.	Under pasture.	Under gardens and orchards	Wood and wild lands.	Cash value of farm in	Cash value of farming implement in
Ameliasburgh	330	6	5	45	136	105	33	39913	26037	18753	6758	526	13876	116830	41067
Athol	209	7	6	18	104	61	13	23391	15088	9894	4945	349	8303	541182	19184
Hallowell	369	19	8	38	145	130	29	41765	28014	14994	11767	253	13751	1392270	41393
Hillier	264	1	1	23	107	115	17	32975	24664	16527	7691	446	8311	1139826	34349
Marysburgh	438	12	11	55	235	103	22	46442	28191	18143	9134	914	18251	1057178	43666
Picton, Town of	9	1	....	2	4	2	....	852	561	299	257	5	291	68300	1065
Sophiasburg	284	.	2	13	110	115	44	42603	28176	19393	8106	672	14432	983578	38973
Total of Prince Edward.	1903	46	33	194	841	631	158	227941	150726	99003	48558	3165	77215	6289164	219697

RETURN OF AGRICULTURAL PRODUCE FOR 1861.—*Continued.*

TOWNSHIPS, &c.	Produce of garden and orchards in	Quantity of land held by Townspeople, not being farmers.	Fall wheat.		Spring wheat.		Barley.		Rye.		Pease.		Oats.	
			Acres.	Bushels.	Acres.	Bushels.	Acres.	Bushels.	Acres.	Bushels.	Acres.	Bushels.	Acres.	Bushels.
Ameliasburgh	11410	250	462	3242	1355	29625	1573	46587	3399	52476	3523	71960	1045	38161
Athol	4222	25	349	3128	829	12786	665	17451	1905	29648	1641	40392	581	18364
Hallowell	5432	297	150	1501	1857	36479	2268	66847	2891	44567	3742	95863	1497	54539
Hillier	5209	180	443	437	1786	31555	3532	93006	2464	32071	3573	79914	1149	36577
Marysburgh	15147	86	161	1417	2677	44514	860	21603	3731	33038	3563	64722	1305	37147
Picton, Town of		90			64	1040	30	874	58	1900	47	905	50	1995
Sophiasburgh	8061	85	125	946	1244	23800	1692	59957	2882	56344	3655	75397	876	31940
Total of Prince Edward	49481	1013	1690	14581	9812	179799	15620	30225	17330	249544	19244	429153	6494	218723

RETURN OF AGRICULTURAL PRODUCE FOR 1861.—*Continued.*

TOWNSHIPS, &c.	Buckwheat.		Indian corn.		Potatoes.		Turnips.		Carrots, Bushels.	Wurzel mang.		Beans, Bushels.	Clover, Timothy and other Grass Seeds,—Bushels.	Hay, Tons.
	Acres.	Bushels.	Acres.	Bushels.	Acres.	Bushels.	Acres.	Bushels.		Acres.	Bushels.			
Ameliasburgh............	1976	46754	917	22440	399	38785	19	6651	9125	1	6893	139	53	2115
Athol...................	799	15857	559	11282	237	21127	15	3723	5169	1	326	117	122	1024
Hallowell	1275	30335	939	26521	451	43675	21	5332	7479	2	1070	148	218	2676
Hillier.................	1843	35039	1020	23185	400	37295	41	6650	3851	4	517	218	823	1656
Marysburgh	2135	49252	713	18755	484	42478	18	4418	1771	1	453	201	203	2428
Picton, Town of........	23	380	17	290	17	1320	......	......	980	3	540	......	......	23
Sophiasburg	1782	42437	908	23055	283	22737	45	4080	3631	1	526	179	387	2637
Total of Prince Edward.	9833	220054	5023	125528	2283	207417	159	30864	32006	13	4115	1002	1806	12559

RETURN OF AGRICULTURAL PRODUCE FOR 1861.—*Continued.*

TOWNSHIPS, &c.	Hops, lbs.	Maple Sugar, lbs.	Cider, Galls.	Wool, lbs.	Fulled Cloth, yds.	Flannel, yds.	Flax and Hemp, lbs.	Linen, yds.	Live Stock.					
									Bulls, Oxen and Steers.	Milch Cows.	Calves and Heifers.	Horses over 3 years old.	Value of same in Dollars.	Colts and fillies.
Ameliasburgh	......	49848	3573	13148	2880	5344	1970	......	289	1575	1256	1190	70508	410
Athol..............	8	26297	4806	7654	1106	5129	170	20	121	724	828	628	40280	206
Hallowell	9200	51461	14446	14218	2126	7354	161	73	143	1626	1301	1202	84838	441
Hillier	46	31821	6870	11561	2214	5431	20	......	216	1218	789	1033	68930	310
Marysburgh	10	31862	1247	15266	1680	10262	30	6	187	1776	1638	1224	79503	433
Picton, Town of......	......	1665	50	38	......	......	......	......	2	196	6	175	......	1
Sophiasburgh	34500	25866	9845	14203	2057	6098	222	11	234	1379	1278	1178	80844	431
Total of Prince Edward.	43764	218820	40837	76098	11463	40118	2573	110	1191	8494	7596	6630	424903	2232

RETURN OF AGRICULTURAL PRODUCE FOR 1861.—*Continued.*

TOWNSHIPS, &c.	Live Stock. Sheeps.	Pigs.	Total value of Live Stock.	Butter, lbs.	Cheese, lbs.	Beef in Bbls. of 200 lbs.	Pork in Bbls. of 200 lbs.	Fish. Salted and Bbl'd.	Sole fresh, lbs.	Carriages kept for pleasure.	Value of same in Dollars	Carriages kept for hire.	Value of same in Dollars.
Ameliasburgh	4337	1483	147688	118671	6038	328	1110	394	3700	570	23297		
Athol	2077	606	76065	45440	3601	144	419	958	3400	253	11710		
Hallowell	4530	1276	131435	103303	84589	103	902	637	3500	660	30186		
Hillier	3587	930	127222	80080	8354	255	1012	1020	3690	518	22643	8	635
Marysburgh	4554	1618	162929	128889	3606	378	1305	784	1564	520	21231		
Picton, Town of	75	152	16451	275		1	14			117	7351	22	995
Sophiasburgh	4706	1320	134686	56165	24413	286	792	199	65	505	24730	1	60
Total of Prince Edward	23866	7385	796476	532823	80601	1495	5554	3992	15919	3125	141148	31	1695

c

METEOROLOGICAL TABLE.

By a careful daily observation made at 6 o'clock A. M. and at 1 and
6 P. M., during the last nine years, in the Village of Bloomfield, five
miles west of Picton, by Levi Varney, the following annual average
temperature is obtained. Thermometer always in the shade at the north
side of the house :—

Year.	Mean.	Highest.	Lowest.	Range.	RMEMARKS.
1857	44.25°	86°	— 25o	111°	The lowest temperature is
1858	45.29°	88°	— 7°	95°	below zero, indicated by the
1859	45.15°	91°	— 19°	110°	sign (—) *minus*.
1860	46.06°	86°	— 14°	100°	The observation in 1865 ex-
1861	45.44°	87°	— 29°	116°	tends through only 11 months.
1862	45.81°	90°	— 7°	97°	They are consequently omitted.
1863	46.10°	91°	— 20°	111°	
1864	46.43°	92°	— 16°	108°	
1865	48.19°	...	......	....	

The annual depth of rain can be obtained for only six years,
commencing with 1860, as follows, viz. :—

Year.	Inches.	Year.	Inches.
1860	27.12	1863	27.59
1861	36.93	1864	35.32
1862	24.13	1865	22.53—11 mos.

10TH BATTALION VOLUNTEER INFANTRY.

Headquarters, Picton.

Lieutenant-Colonel Commanding—W. Ross, M.P.P.; Major, Thomas
Bog; Adjutant-Surgeon, J. C. Rankin. Left limits.

No. 1 Company, Picton.—Captain, D. Fraser; Lieutenant, G. A
Simpson, temporary ; Ensign, A. J. Wright.

No. 2 Company, Picton.—Captain, J. W. Langmuir; Lieutenant,
G. B. Dougall, temporary ; Ensign, W. J. Hare.

No. 3 Company, Wellington.—Captain, William Patterson ; Lieutenant, vacant ; Ensign, vacant.

No. 4 Company, Consecon.—Captain, Edward Brady; Lieutenant,
Thomas Thurresson; Ensign, G. B. Johnson.

No. 5 Company, Milford.— Captain, J. C. Lake; Lieutenant, J. H.
Ackerman ; Ensign, Richard Ostrander.

No. 6 Company, Milford.—Captain, Joseph Clapp; Lieutenant,
Donald Ross ; Ensign, Edward Dulmadge.

No. 7 Company, Picton.—Captain, J. H. Allan; Lieutenant, W.
McKenzie ; Ensign, Frederick White.

Drill Instructor, Major Bog.

COUNTY INFORMATION.

MEMBERS OF PARLIAMENT.

Hon. Robert Read, Member of the Legislative Council for the Quinte Division.

Walter Ross, Esquire, Member for the Legislative Council for the County of Prince Edward.

MEMBERS OF COUNTY COUNCIL.

Samuel Sprague,.....Ameliasburg.	John Pringer,.........Marysburgh.
James Young,.......... "	A. Greeley,...........Sophiasburgh.
S. P. Niles,...........Hillier.	Peter Wood,.......... "
Richard Noxon,....... "	Robert Kelly,.........Athol.
R. R. Burlingham,..Hallowell.	Thomas Stramon,...Picton.
Henry Hubles,......... "	Donald Campbell,...Wellington
Philip Clapp,..........Marysburgh.	

COUNTY OFFICERS.

S. P. Niles, Warden, Residence, Hillier.

H. J. Thorp, Sheriff, Office, Main Street, Picton.

D. D. Fairfield, Esquire, Judge of County and Surrogate Courts, and Chairman Quarter Sessions, Chambers opposite " Steam Boat Hotel," Picton.

John P. Roblin, Registrar, Main Street, Picton.

John S. Clute, Deputy Registrar, Main Street, Picton.

Philip Low, Esquire, Clerk of the Peace and Crown, Attorney, Office, Main Street, Picton.

Johh Twigg, Clerk County Court, Deputy Clerk of the Crown, and Registrar Surrogate Court, Office, Main Street, Picton.

Robert Boyle, County Clerk, Office, " *Times Office.*"

R. J. Chapman, County Treasurer, Office, Main Street, Picton.

James B. Lay, Sheriff's Bail ff.

John O. Conger, County Surveyor, Office, " *Picton Gazette.*"

Henry McDonald, Jailer.

William Anderson, Turnkey.

DIVISION COURT CLERKS.

John P. Downs, Clerk 1st Division Court, Office, Main Street, Picton.

James Cook, Clerk 2nd Division Court, Milford.

Samuel Solmes, Clerk 3rd Division Court, Northport.

Edward Roblin, Clerk 4th Division Court, Roblin's Mills.
William Young, Clerk 5th Division Court, Wellington.
Harvey Spafford, Clerk 6th Division Court, Cherry Valley.
John M. Cadman, Clerk 7th Division Court, Consecon.
Richard Hill, Clerk 8th Division Court, Bongard's Corners.

CORONERS.

Dr. Evans.   Dr. Moore.   Dr. Young of Picton.

COURTS FOR 1866.

QUARTER SESSIONS.

13th March ; 12th June ; 11th September ; 11th December.

COUNTY COURT.

TERMS.

DIVISION COURTS.

PRINCE EDWARD AGRICULTURAL SOCIETY.

Officers for 1865.—William Ross, President; D. Baker, 1st Vice President ; J. Cavan, 2nd Vice-President ; J. P. Roblin, Secretary and Treasurer.

Sam. Jones, Wm. Anderson, W. J. Boulter, Robt. Clapp, Thos. Bog, John Murray, W. N. Bedall.—Directors.

The Annual Meeting is held the third week in January.

Phœnix Temple, Independent Order of Good Templars, No. 275, organized October 5, 1864, meet every week on Friday evening, at 7½ o'clock. Names of officers for quarter commencing Nov. 1, 1865 :—

William Smeaton,	W. C. S.
Francis Dunn,	W. V. S.
E. W. Morse,	W. S.
Eyre Randall.	W. S.
Arthur V. Dunn,	W. M.
George McMullen,	W. J. G.
Mary Mitchell	R. H. S.
Jane Allison,	L. H. S.
John M. Platt,	W. C.
Martha Wright,	W. A. S.
John Twigg,	W. F. S.
Harriett Green,	W. D. M.
Timothy Gorman,	W. O. C.

MASONIC.

This District is composed of the Counties of Prince Edward, Hastings, Lennox and Addington, and Renfrew.

PICTON.

Prince Edward Lodge, No. 18.

OFFICERS :

J. N. Carter,..........................W. M.
Lucius Hart,..........................S. W.
A. J. Corkindale.................... .J. W.
Thomas Shannon,.....................Secretary.
David Barker,........................ Treasurer.

Meets on Thursday each month, on or preceding full moon.

WELLINGTON.

Star in the East Lodge, No. 164.

OFFICERS :

Donald Ross,..........................W. M.
S. W. Flager,.............. ....S. W.
William Patterson,....................J. W.
William Clemenson ....Secretary.
William Harris,...................... Treasurer.

Meets on Thursday each month, on or preceding full moon.

Consecon Lodge, No. 50.

A. R. McDonald, ...W. M.
———— ....S. W.
———— ....J. W.
A. G. Whittier,........................Secretary.
———— ....Treasurer.

Meets on Friday each month, on or preceding full moon.

BY-LAWS OF THE COUNTY OF PRINCE EDWARD.

BY-LAW No. 1.—IMPOSING PENALTIES.

I. That any Officer duly appointed by the Municipal Corporation of the County of Prince Edward, and who has accepted such appointment, and taken and subscribed the necessary Oath of Office, who shall neglect or refuse to perform the duties of his Office, as prescribed by Statute or any By-Law in force in the said County; or who shall neglect or refuse to execute, when required, any order or Resolution of the said Corporation pertaining to his said Office, shall forfeit and pay a sum not exceeding Fifty Dollars for every such neglect or refusal—and in default of payment to be imprisoned in the Common Gaol of the said County, for a period (at hard labor) not exceeding Twenty-one Days.—22 *Vic., Cap.* 54, *Sec.* 243.

II. Any person refusing to obey any of the By-Laws of this Corporation, or contravening any of their provisions, or any lawful order or Resolution of this Corporation, shall incur the same penalty as is mentioned in the preceding Section of this By-Law. Such penalties to be recovered and enforced on complaint of the proper Municipal Officer, or any inhabitant of the County, in a summary way, before any Magistrate of the County, by Warrant under his hand and seal, in accordance with the directions contained in the Act 17 Vic., Cap. 178; and unless otherwise specially directed the fines shall be paid over by such Magistrate into the County Treasury, for the general purposes of the County.

III. It shall not be necessary, in any subsequent By-Law of this Corporation, to enact any penal provisions—but reference shall be had to the mode of proceeding set forth in this By-Law, which is intended to apply to every By-Law, order and Resolution of this Corporation.

[Passed November 25th, 1862.]

N. BALLARD, County Clerk.   G. STRIKER, Warden.

BY-LAW No. 2.—SALARIES OF COUNTY OFFICERS.

I. That the Members of this Council shall receive the sum of One Dollar and Fifty Cents for each day spent in attending to the business of the Corporation.—22 *Vic., Cap.* 54, *Sec.* 269.

II. The Clerk of this Council shall receive the sum of Seventy-five Dollars each year, for his services as Clerk, which shall include all the duties appertaining to his Office that may be imposed on him by this Council or by any Statute now in force in this Province, or that may be in force.—22 *Vic., Cap.* 54, *Sec.* 173.

III. The Salary of the Treasurer shall be Two Hundred and Forty Dollars per Annum, commencing on and after the thirty-first day of December next.—22 *Vic., Cap.* 54, *Sec.* 174.

IV. The Auditors shall receive the sum of Five Dollars each, per Annum, for their services.—22 *Vic., Cap.* 54, *Section* 173.

V. The Surgeon of the Gaol shall be paid the sum of Thirty Dollars, per Annum, for his services.—22. *Vic., Cap.* 53, *Secs.* 173 and 284.

[Passed November 25th, 1872.]

N. BALLARD, Clerk.   G. STRIKER, Warden.

BY-LAW No. 3.—JURORS.

I. That every Grand Juror shall receive the sum of One Dollar for each day's attendance at the Sittings of any of Her Majesty's Courts of Criminal Jurisdiction in this County.—22 *Vic., Cap.* 31, *Sec.* 140.

II. That every Petit Juror shall receive Ten Cents per Mile, for every Mile necessarily travelled to attend any of Her Majesty's Courts of Civil or Criminal Jurisdiction; and One Dollar per day for each day's attendance at the Sittings of any such Courts.—22 *Vic.*, *Cap.* 31, *Sec.* 141.

III. The Sheriff of this County shall receive the sum of Fifty Cents for checking the names of the Jurors, at the opening of the Court, on each day; and One Dollar for certifying and returning such List to the Treasurer—which sums shall be paid him on the or derof the Magistrates in Session.—22 *Vic.*, *Cap.* 31, *Sec.* 145.

[Passed 25th November, 1862.

N. BALLARD, County Clerk.   G. STRIKER, Warden.

BY-LAW No. 4.—INSPECTOR OF WEIGHTS AND MEASURES.

I. That one Inspector of Weights and Measures shall be appointed in this County, but whose jurisdiction shall not extend to the Town of Picton.

II. He shall attend at the Town of Picton, during the first **week of** April and September, for the purpose of examining such **weights and** measures as may be brought him; and shall give such notice as directed, and be guided in all respects by the provisions of Chapter 58 of the Consolidated Statutes of Upper Canada.

N. BALLARD, County Clerk.   G. STRIKER, Warden.

BY-LAW No. 5.—PUBLIC MORALS.

I. That the penalties mentioned in By-Law No. One may be enforced in the mamer therein set forth, against every person who shall—

1st—Hunt, fish, play at any games, or perform any labor, except carrying passengers, Her Majesty's Mails, or works of necessity and of charity, on the Sabbath day.—22 *Vic.*, *Cap.* 54, *Sec.* 282.

2nd—Or who shall sell or give intoxicating drink to a child, apprentice, or servant, without the consent of a parent, master or legal protector.

3rd—Or who shall post indecent placards, writings or pictures, or write indecent words, or make indecent pictures or drawings on walls or fences, in streets or public places.

4th—Or who shall be guilty of any drunkenness, profane swearing, obscene, blasphemous, or grossly insulting language, and other immorality and indecency in streets, highways and public places.

5th—Or who shall keep a tippling house, or house of ill fame.

6th—Or who shall keep a gambling house.

7th—Or who shall be found begging, or drunk, or disorderly, in any street, highway or public place, within the County.

8th— Or who shall indecently expose the person, publicly, or wash or bathe the person, in any public water, near a public Highway.

9th—Or who shall race horses on any highway, common, or any ice, within the jurisdiction of this County.

N. BALLARD, County Clerk.   G. STRIKER, Warden.

BY-LAW No. 6.—AUCTIONEERS, HAWKERS AND PEDLARS.

I. That the penalties enacted in By-Law No. One, in the manner therein directed, may be enforced against any person who shall—

1st—Sell, or offer for sale, as an Auctioneer, any goods, wares, and merchandize, other than the estate of a deceased person, or which may be sold under an execution issued out of any of Her Majesty's Courts, or Distress Warrant, or the Warrant of a Board of School Trustees, without having first obtained a license from the proper Officer, as hereinafter mentioned (22 *Vic., Cap.* 54, *Sec.* 284, *Sub Sec.* 2.) or

2nd—Who shall offer for sale, or sell, any goods, wares or merchandize, by travelling from house to house, either on foot or with a horse or horses, or other beast of burthen, or with any boat, vessel, or craft, such person not having become a permanent resident of the County, or householder therein, without having first obtained a License from the proper Officer.— (*Sub Sec.* 3.)

II. The Clerk of this Corporation shall issue a License to every person applying for the same, to enable him to act as an Auctioneer, on the receipt of twelve dollars; which License shall not be transferable, and which shall remain in force for one year from the date, except as hereinafter provided.

III. The Clerk shall also issue a License to every person applying for the same, on the receipt of Six Dollars, authorizing such person to carry goods from house to house, and offer them for sale, by travelling on foot ; for every horse or beast bearing or drawing a burthen, an additional sum of Six Dollars ; for every decked vessel, on board of which goods are exposed for sale, Twenty Dollars—and for every boat or craft used as above, Ten Dollars.

IV. The Licenses shall be signed by the Warden, and countersigned by the Clerk. They shall be in force for one year, or a specified portion of a year, not less than six months from the date. In which case the amount to be paid shall bear the same proportion to the whole amount as the part of the year for which a License is obtained does to the whole year.

V. All moneys coming into the hands of the Clerk, for Licenses, shall be by him paid over, forthwith, to the County Treasurer.

VI. All blank Licenses, signed by the Warden, shall be numbered by him, and corresponding numbers entered in a book to be kept by him, and when moneys for Licenses shall be paid over by the Clerk, to the County Treasurer, the numbers of the Licenses shall also be designated and appear on the Treasurer's Books.

N. BALLARD, County Clerk.   G. STRIKER, Warden

BY-LAW No. 7.—BY-LAW TO OPEN ROAD.

Whereas the allowance for Road between the First Concession produced in the Township of Sophiasburgh, and a part of the Second Concession produced in the Township of Hallowell, from the limits between Lots number sixty and sixty-one, to the limits between sixty-four and sixty-five, in the said Second Concession produced, has been for a long time travelled, but has never been opened to the full width as originally laid out, and whereas it is necessary to open it to its full width—

Therefore, the Municipal Corporation of the County of Prince Edward enacts:

I. That the Road from the limit between Lots number sixty-one and sixty-two, in the Second Concession produced, of the Township of Sophiasburgh, to the line between Lots number sixty-four and sixty-five, formerly in Sophiasburgh, now in the Township of Hallowell, be made sixty-six feet wide from the front of the said Second Concession produced.

II. *Be it further enacted,* That it shall be the duty of the County Engineer to ascertain the front line of the said Second Concession produced, between the limits indicated, if the said line be not now ascertained, and lay off the Road sixty-six feet in width from the said front line of the Second Concession produced, and plant posts between the allowance for Road and the First Concession produced of Sophiasburgh aforesaid.

III. *Be it further enacted,* That written notice be given by the Engineer to all parties found in possession of said Road allowance, or any part of it, requiring them to remove their fences from off the allowance for Road.

IV. Any person or persons neglecting or refusing to obey the requirements of this By-Law shall be prosecuted as provided in By-Law No. 1.

N. BALLARD, Clerk.   G. STRIKER, Warden

BY-LAW No. 8—WELLINGTON INCORPORATION.

Whereas, by the Census Returns of the Village of Wellington, in the Townships of Hillier and Hallowell, in this County, it appears that there are over Seven Hundred and Fifty inhabitants within the limits of said Village; and whereas, One Hundred of the Freeholders and House-holders within such limits have petitioned this Council to pass a By-Law incorporating said Village; and whereas, it is only just and proper to comply with the request contained in the petition—

Therefore, the Municipal Corporation of the County of Prince Edward enacts:

I. That so much of the Townships of Hillier and Hallowell as is contained within the following boundaries, shall be designated the Village of Wellington; and shall, from and after the time when this By-Law takes effect, be incorporated under the above name, according to the intent and meaning of the Statute 22 Vic., Chap. 54, Section 10—

Commencing at the Lake Shore of Lake Ontario, on the West side of Lot No. 7, in the First Concession of the Township of Hillier; thence along the West boundary line of said Lot to the rear; thence along the rear of said Lot, and along the rear of Lots numbers 6, 5, 4, and 3 ; thence along the rear of those parts of Lots No. 2 and 1 as at present owned or occupied by Daniel Reynolds, J. T. Dorland, and Joseph Cummins, to the Township line between Hillier and Hallowell; thence along the rear of those parts of Lots Nos. 1 and 2, in the Township of Hallowell, as occupied by Patrick MacKessy, Joseph Cummins, and Francis W. Mandeville, to the East boundary of said Lot No. 2 in the Township of Hallowell; thence along said East boundary line of Lot No. 2 to the waters of the West Lake; thence along the water-line of said West Lake and of Lake Ontario, to the place of beginning.

II. The first Election to be held at the Town Hall in said Village, and John T. Dorland shall be Returning Officer.

III. This By-Law shall take effect on and after the Twentieth of December next.

[Passed 30th October, 1862.]

N. BALLARD, Clerk   G. STRIKER, Warden.

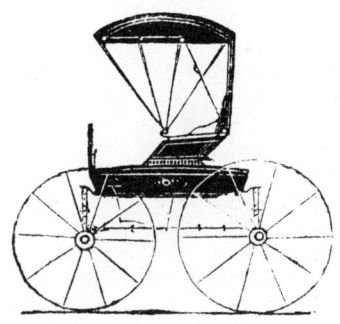

TOWN OF PICTON, CO. PRINCE EDWARD.

(First settlement on Delhi side of Bay in Tavern kept by —.)

From the records in possession of the Town Clerk, we find on the 21st January, 1850, at a meeting of the Board of Police of the Town of Picton, held at the C.H., the following councillors for said Town were present, and handed in their oath of qualification, and also their oath of office.

For Hallowell Ward—Wm. Hale, James McDonald, and Calvin Pier, Esqs.

" Brock do. —David Barker Stevenson, Jas. Porter, and Walter Ross, Esqs.

" Tecumseth do. —John Proctor, P.ilip Low, and John Miller, Esqs,

Moved by Mr. Hale, seconded by Mr. Ross, and carried unanimously. that Mr. Low be appointed Mayor of this Council. Lempriere Murray was appointed Clerk. At a meeting held next day, Cecil Mortimer was appointed Auditor by Mayor in Council, James Cook was also appointed Auditor on behalf of Council, Jno. G. Reynolds, chief constable of Town. Three subs were appointed, one for each ward. David Barker Stevenson was appointed Town Reeve to represent the Town in Council. Lampriere Murray was appointed Treasurer of Town. James Shannon, Weigh Master. J. G. Reynolds, Collector of Rates. After the appointment of local committees, the Council adjourned.

The Council met on Thursday, the 26th day of December, by special appointment, when, on motion of Mr. Stevenson, the Council passed the following resolution : That the death of Mr. Councillor Hale deprives this Board of an esteemed member, and suggests the duty of recording the high sense it entertains of his characteristic sincerity and benevolent disposition as a man, and viewing his valuable services for several years as a member for Hallowell Ward, his loss will be long felt by the Town, and that therefore it be resolved : That this Ward have the melancholy satisfaction of recording this tribute to his memory.

From the same record we further find, that on the seventeenth day of January, 1857, one half of the taxes paid by certain parties was returned on account of their having suffered by a fire, and not being insured. Also, that sick emigrants occupied a house, the property of Hubbs & Wilson, for which they, H. & W., received the sum of ten dollars from the Town Council.

The Council for the Town in 1851 were W. T. Yarwood, M. W. Morse, and Calvin Pier, for Hallowell Ward ; Thos. More, D. B. Stevenson, and L. Walla, for Brock Ward ; Francis G. Owens, Philip Low, and Jno. Mill, for Tecumseth Ward. Mr. Low was appointed Mayor in opposition to Thos. Moore, by the casting vote of the Mayor, and Mr. Stevens elected Town Reeve by same vote. 1852 the Councillors elected for the Town were, Brock Ward : D. B. Stevenson, B. McFaul, and Luke Wallace ; for Hallowell Ward : Rufus Lawyer, Calvin Pier, and Thos. Yarwood ; Tecumseth Ward : Philip Low, Cecil Mortimer, Francis L.

Owens. Mr. Philip Low was appointed Mayor. D. B. Stevenson Town Reeve.

The Councillors elected for the Town, 1853, for Hallowell Ward : Archibald Purdy Babbitt, Calvin Pier, Chas. Stewart Wilson ; for Brock Ward : R. Ramsay, D. B. Stevenson, R. Leatch ; for Tecumseth Ward : F. G. Owens, Ph. Low, Cecil Mortimer. Mr. Ph. Low was elected Mayor. D. B. Stevenson Reeve.

The Councillors elected for 18:4 were, for Hallowell Ward : A. P. Babbitt, Chas. S. Wilson, W. T. Yarwood ; Brock Ward : Stewart Wilson, D. B. Stevenson ; Tecumseth Ward : F. G. Owens, Cecil Mortimer, James Miller. D. B. Stevenson was elected Mayor. C. S. Wilson, Reeve. The resignation of Mr. Murray as Clerk and Treasurer was then handed in and received. Moved by Mr. Yarwood, and seconded by C. S. Wilson, that John Twigg be appointed Clerk and Treasurer—Carried. The Council for the Town in 1855 were, for Tecumseth Ward : Cecil Mortimer, F. G. Owens, Wm. Owens ; Tecumseth Ward : Stewart Wilson, R. Ramsay, Jas. Porter ; Hallowell Ward : C. S. Wilson, A. P. Babbitt, W. T. Yarwood. Cecil Mortimer Mayor ; R. Ramsay, Reeve.

The Councillors elected for 1856 : Tecumseth Ward—F. G. Owens, J.W. Langmuir, Wm. Owens ; Brock Ward : R. Ramsay, Thos. Donnelly, Walter Ross ; Hallowell Ward : W. T. Yarwood, A. P. Babbitt, Jas. Gillespie, jun. F. G. Owens, Mayor. R. Ramsay, Reeve. The Councillors for 1857. Hallowell Ward : W. T. Yarwood. Jas. McDonald, Jas. Gillespie, jun. ; Brock Ward : R. Ramsay, Gideon Striker, Walter Ross ; Tecumseth Ward : J. W. Langmuir, F. G. Owens, Wm. Owens. R. Ramsay, Mayor. W. T. Yarwood, Reeve. The Councillors for 1858. Hallowell Ward : Chas. S. Wilson, W. T. Yarwood, G. C. Curry ; Brock Wark : Gideon Striker, James Wycott, Wm. McGowan ; Tecumseth Ward : F. G. Owens, Wm. Owens, James Jamieson. C. S. Wilson, Mayor. W. T. Yarwood, Reeve. The Councillors for 1859. Hallowell Ward : C. S. Wilson, W. T. Yarwood, G C. Curry ; Brock Ward : G. Striker, Thos. McFaul, Wm. McGowan ; Tecumseth Ward : Wm. Owens, James Jamieson, James Mulholland. R. Ramsay, Mayor. It was in this year the Mayor was elected by the voice of the people. G. Striker, Reeve. Councillors for 1860. Hallowell Ward : W. P. Ketchum, Geo. H. Hart, Jas. Wycott ; Brock Ward : G. Striker, Wm. McGowan, A. Patterson ; Tecumseth Ward : J. W. Langmuir, Wm. Owens, Jas. Jamieson. W. Ross, Mayor. W. P. Ketchum, Reeve. Councillors for 1861. Hallowell Ward : W. P. Ketchum, Jas. Gillespie, W. T. Yarwood ; Brock Ward : Thos. McFaul. Thos. Shannon, Thos. Bag ; Tecumseth Ward : Wm. Owens, J. W. Langmuir, Jas. Jamieson. J. W. Langmuir, Reeve. Council for 1862. Hallowell Ward : W. T. Yarwood, G. C. Curry, W. C. Ingersoll ; Brock Ward : G. Striker, J. W. Langmuir, R. Ramsay ; Tecumseth Ward : Jas. Jamieson, Wm. Owens, J. Mullholland. W. Ross, Mayor. G. Striker, Reeve. The Council for 1863. Hallowell Ward : W. T. Yarwood, G. Curry, W. P. Reynolds ; Brock Ward : G. Striker, J. W. Langmuir, Jno. Vance ; Tecumseth Ward : W. Owens,

Jas. Mulholland, Jas. Jamieson. G. Striker, Reeve; G. C. Curry, Deputy Reeve. The Councillors for 1864. Hallowell Ward : W. P. Reynolds, Geo. H. Hart, J. H. Allen ; Brock Ward : G. Striker, Jno. Vance, Jacob J. Fralick ; Tecumseth Ward : Wm. Owens, Jas. Mulholland, James Jamieson. J. W. Langmuir, Mayor. G. Striker, Reeve. The Council for 1865. Hallowell Ward : G. H. Hart, J. H. Allan, W. P. Reynolds; Brock Ward : R. A. Norman, Thos. Shannon; Tecumseth Ward : Jas. Jamieson, Jas. Mulholland, Jas. Rolston. Thos. Shannon, Reeve. Wm. Owens, Mayor.

A SYNOPSIS OF THE BY-LAWS OF THE TOWN OF PICTON.

BY-LAW No. 1.

To Provide for the Preservation of Peace, Order and good Government in the Town of Picton.

CLAUSE 1 enacts that no person shall injure, deface or damage any Town property, or make any disturbance in any place of Public Worship, or inscribe or draw indecent words or pictures on any wall, fence, or other public place, or be guilty of drunkenness, or make use of profane or insulting language, or destroy any trees which serve to ornament the streets, or be guilty of indecent exposure of person.

CLAUSE 2 prohibits public exhibitions, &c., unless licensed by the Mayor, who is thereby authorised to issue such license, charging for the same any sum not exceeding Twenty Dollars.

CLAUSE 3 places the power in the Mayor's hands of permitting lectures to be given, or prohibiting the same.

CLAUSE 9 fixes the weight of a Baker's loaf of bread sold in the town, at four pounds avoirdupois, smaller loaves to weigh in proportion : makes it the duty of the chief constable to examine the same, and of the Mayor or Clerk to punish by forfeiture parties who may be guilty of selling light loaves.

CLAUSE 10 prohibits gaming, and orders all devices used for that purpose to be seized and destroyed.

CLAUSE 15 confers on the members of the council the same power as that of the chief-constable, so far as the apprehension of offenders is concerned.

BY-LAW No. 2.

Provides Allowance to and defines the duties of certain Officers of the Town.

CLAUSE 1.—That the Town Treasurer, before entering on his official duties, shall deposit with the Mayor his bond for the sum of Two Thousand Dollars, and two sufficient sureties in the sum of one thousand five hundred dollars each, conditional for the due and faithful discharge of the duties appertaining to his office.

CLAUSE 2.—That the Treasurer shall receive all the revenues of the Town. Such monies can only be withdrawn and paid out by resolution of the Council, a copy of which, certified by the Clerk, and signed by the Mayor or Chairman, shall be his authority. And the Treasurer shall keep a regular sett of books, which he shall, when requested to do so, hand over to his successor in office, together with all papers and moneys belonging thereto.

CLAUSE 3.—The Treasurer shall receive Sixty Dollars per annum as salary.

CLAUSE 4.—That the Collector, before receiving his Roll, shall furnish the same security as the Treasurer, depositing with the Treasurer all moneys collected by him on the Collector's Roll; at no time retaining in his hands a sum in excess of Four Hundred Dollars, without making a deposit of the same. The Collector's property qualification to be the same as a Town Councillor.

CLAUSE 6.—Collector's salary to be Seventy-Five dollars per year, payable when his duties are performed.

CLAUSE 7.—The Assessor to perform his duties according to law, receiving a salary of Fifty Dollars per annum.

CLAUSE 8.—It shall be the duty of the Clerk to make out a Collector's Roll, specifying the rate of Taxes for all purposes separately, certifying to the correctness of the same, it to be delivered to the Collector on or before the First of October in each year.

CLAUSE 10.—Clerk to act in that capacity at the Police Court, depositing the balance that may remain on hand at the end of the year, with the Treasurer.

CLAUSE 11.—Clerk's salary, One Hundred Dollars per year, payable half-yearly.

CLAUSE 12.—That there be one Chief-Constable, who shall follow the directions of the Council, apprehending parties guilty of committing any act against the Town By-Laws. He is empowered to turn over such offenders to the keeper of the Common Goal, who is thereby authorized to receive and confine the same, subject to orders.

CLAUSE 13.—Chief Constable's salary to be Two Hundred Dollars per annum, together with the usual constable's fee.—Said salary payable quarterly.

CLAUSE 14.—One Inspector of Shop and Tavern Licenses shall be appointed by the Council yearly, his term of office to expire at the end of the current year, property qualification to be the same as a Councillor.

CLAUSE 15.—The said Inspector to subscribe to the necessary declarations of office and qualification, and deposit the same with the Clerk within eight days, under the penalty of being guilty of a misdemeanor.

CLAUSE 16.—That the Inspector shall publicly notify all persons intending to present their applications for certificates for Tavern and Shop License, to do so at his usual place of business, on the second Monday in February. He shall then proceed to examine the premises of all applicants, and on the third Monday in the said month grant certificates to those applicants entitled to receive them. Only British subjects shall receive certificates who are of sober life and conversation.

CLAUSE 18.—Salary of Inspector to be Five Dollars per annum. Surety to the amount of Three Hundred Dollars required of him.

CLAUSE 19 appoints one Pound Keeper.

CLAUSE 20 fixes the Returning Officer's salary at Two Dollars per day, while engaged at elections.

CLAUSE 21.—The Auditors shall receive Five Dollars each for their services.

CLAUSE 22 appoints a Weigh Master.

.CLAUSE 23 provides for the annual appointment of three Fence Viewers.

BY-LAW No. 4

Provides for the improvement of Streets, and orders a copy of By-Law to be furnished to non-residents who may be affected thereby.

BY-LAW No. 5,

For the Prevention of Fires.

Prohibits the erection of wooden buildings within the following limits: On Main Street, at the stone monument planted on the westerly side of lot No. 1 ; thence along the northerly side of said street, to Paul Street, on the south side of Main Street, at the south-west side of the lot known as Mortimer's land ; thence along the southerly side of said Main Street to Chapel Street, on both sides of Bridge Street, from Main Street to within one hundred and twenty-five feet of the centre of the Creek. This by-law also prohibits additions being made to any wooden buildings already erected within said limits, unless the same be built of brick or stone, and provides for the prevention of fires generally, and provides for the punishment of parties violating this by-law by fine not to exceed Twenty Dollars per week, but to continue in force till the house or other building, and every part thereof, shall be removed ; it also enacts for the punishment of parties employed as master-builder, mechanic, or laborer, who are to be punished by a fine not exceeding Twenty Dollars, together with all costs and charges for every day he or they shall have been so employed.

BY-LAW No. 6.

CLAUSE 1.—One Chief Fire-Engineer and two Fire-Wardens in each ward of the town, to be appointed annually.

CLAUSE 2.—The Fire-Engineer has full control and chief direction at all fires, the movements of other officers, and the inhabitants are subject to his orders thereat. He can, with the concurrence of any one of the Fire Wardens, order the pulling down or blowing up of any of the adjacent buildings that he may deem necessary for preventing further damage.

CLAUSE 3.—The Fire Wardens shall examine the condition of all tenements and premises within the town once every year in the month of December, with respect to their security against fires, and report thereon to the Council, to give orders to the inhabitants assembled at fires as to their conduct thereat.

CLAUSE 5.—No person shall use a lighted candle in any stable or other building where any combustible materials shall be kept, or shall carry fire through any place or street without securing such fire in a proper manner.

CLAUSE 6.—No person shall place any ashes in any wooden receptacle or otherwise, within twelve feet of any wooden building or fence connected with any such building.

CLAUSE 7.—The owner of any building in which a fire is kept shall have a good and sufficient ladder reaching to the top of the roof. A fine is imposed as penalty for non-compliance.

CLAUSE 8.—No combustible material to be burnt in any street of the town, nor within twenty feet of any building; and no person shall be present aiding or abetting in the same.

CLAUSE 9.—Occupants of premises must cause all chimneys on their premises to be swept and stove-pipes cleaned (if considered necessary by the Inspector) during the months of March and November in each year.

CLAUSE 10.—Orders the appointment of a Chimney Inspector, and orders him to examine into and report on the condition of all chimneys and stove-pipes within the Corporation.

CLAUSE 11.—Enacts that the following tariff for the payment of persons employed as sweepers be established :—

No. 1.—For a chimney one ground floor in height, ten cents. For every additional flue, five cents.

No. 2.—For a chimney higher than No. 1, not exceeding in height two floors and a garret, fifteen cents. Every additional flue, five cents.

No. 3.—For a chimney higher than No. 2, not exceeding three floors and a garret, twenty-five cents. Every additional flue, six cents.

No. 4.—For a chimney higher than No. 3, twenty-five cents. Every additional flue, ten cents ; which charge shall be paid at the time of sweeping by the occupant or occupants of said house.

BY-LAW No. 7.

A By-Law to establish the Scales now laid down on Main Street, as the Public Scales of the Town, and to regulate the weighing of Hay, Straw, and other articles.

CLAUSE 2.—That all hay, straw, or other articles required to be weighed as soon as they are brought into the town, either sold or for sale, shall be weighed at the Public Weight-Scales by the Weight-Master in charge thereof, and any person or persons who shall neglect doing so shall be subject to a penalty.

CLAUSE 4.—The Weigh-Master shall furnish the person or persons having charge of the load so weighed with a weigh-note, dated and signed, stating weight in pounds, with the wagon or other vehicle, the tare of the same, the nett weight of the load, the name of the person having charge, and the name of the purchaser.

CLAUSE 6.—The Weigh-Master shall keep a book in which he shall enter the name of every person for whom he shall weigh any article, the article weighed, and the weight thereof, and the date of weighing; which book shall be open at all reasonable times, for inspection. He shall make a return to the Council at the end of each month, with the fee paid in each case.

CLAUSE 9.—The Weigh-Master shall retain the one half of all fees received by him for his own use, and pay over the other half to the Treasurer of the Town.

CLAUSE 12.—The fees shall be as follows :—

For every load of hay, straw, or other article, and
    return wagon free................................... 20 cents.
For every divided load, each portion so divided....... 15 "
For every other article........ .... 12 "

And all such sums as above shall be paid for before the article or vehicle is taken away.

BY-LAW No. 8

Enacts that no horse, bull, cow, sheep, or cattle of any description, shall run at large in the streets of the Town from the first day of December in each year, to the first day of April in each succeeding year. That no swine, pigs, goats, domestic fowls, or poultry shall run at large at any time. It also makes provision for a pound, and authorises the sale of animals impounded, if dues are not paid and property claimed. The pound-keeper's fees are :—

For each horse or head of cattle impounded......... 15 cents.
   "   sheep, swine, &c.,   "   .... 12½ "
   "   fowl or poultry   "   .... 5 "
For feeding 20 lbs. of hay to each horse or 15 lbs.
    to each head of cattle every 24 hours...... 20 "
   "   5 lbs. of hay to each sheep   "   ..... 10 "
   "   1 pint of peas or corn to each swine every
    24 hours....................................... 10 "
For advertising sale....................................... 25 "
For each sale............................. .... 50 "
For notice to each Fence Viewer..................... 25 "

BY-LAW No. 9

Is designed to restrain dogs from running at large, and imposes a tax thereon of One Dollar on each dog, and Two Dollars on each bitch, the above tax to be collected at the same time and in the same manner as other taxes of the Corporation are done.

BY-LAW No. 10

Provides that the Selectors of Jurors shall receive the following amounts, viz. :—The Clerk, one dollar and fifty cents for each hundred names, and the Mayor and Assessor one dollar for each hundred names, which sums shall be paid by the Treasurer, on the production of the certificate of the Clerk of the Peace, as the law directs.

BY-LAW No. 11.

Board of Health.

1. To be composed of three members of the Council, and three others not connected therewith, to be appointed annually by the Council.

2. At least one member of the Board to be a medical practitioner.

3. That no person shall suffer the accumulation of any dung, manure, offal. filth, refuse, stagnant water, or other matter, on his or other premises, or on any vacant lot in the town, so as to be a nuisance or injurious to the health of any person in the town.

The Board of Health are empowered to direct any of their officers to enter any building or premises in the day-time, on the receipt by them of a complaint signed by one or more inhabitants of the town, and to cause to be removed (if necessary) anything therein which is prejudicial to health. and if any proprietor or representative having control of such premises, after having had twenty-four hours' notice from such officer of the Board of Health to remove such nuisance, shall neglect or refuse to do so, he, she or they, shall be subject to a penalty.

BY-LAW No. 14

Enacts that any person who is convicted of a breach of any of the By-Laws of the Corporation, and neglects to pay the fine or penalty within the time specified in the conviction or order, shall be committed to the Common Gaol of the County for any period not exceeding twenty-one days, with or without hard labor ; or a distress warrant against the goods and chattels of such offender may issue at the end of the time allowed for the payment of the fine or penalty, and costs of prosecution, and in case of sufficient goods or chattels not being found, be committed to the Common Gaol for any period not exceeding twenty-one days, with or without hard labor.

TAKEN FROM THE STANDING RULES OF THE TOWN COUNCIL OF THE TOWN OF PICTON.

The Council shall meet on the first Monday in each month, at the hour of seven o'clock, P. M., unless such Monday shall be a public holiday according to law, when the Council shall meet on the next day following, which shall not be such public Holiday.

The Council may adjourn for want of a quorum, if enough members are not present to constitute one, one hour after the regular time of meeting.

The Mayor shall preside, or the Reeve in his absence, and in, the absence of both, the Council shall select one of their members.

The Clerk shall take down the names of the members present, and read the minutes of the last regular meeting and of any special meeting intervening, in order that any mistakes therein may be corrected.

The ordinary routine of the Council shall be : —

> 1st. Presenting Petitions.
> 2nd. Reading Petitions.
> 3rd. " Communications.
> 4th. " Reports of Committees.
> 5th. Unfinished Business.
> 6th. Motions.

And that all Business shall be taken up in regular order.

PICTON.

Picton contains two Iron Foundries. Barker & Shannon's Foundry is situated on Elizabeth Street, and is owned by David Barker, Esquire, and carried on by Thomas Shannon. The machinery is propelled by Steam power. This foundry has been established for many years, and contains the very best kind of machinery—some designed and manufactured by the proprietors. They employ ten hands, and turn out steam engines, lathes, agricultural implements, saw and grist mill machinery of every description, stoves, &c.

Phœnix Foundry is situated on Mary Street, and is owned by Stewart Wilson, and carried on by John McGregor & Co.; the machinery is propelled by steam. They employ five hands. Agricultural implements and stoves are the chief articles manufactured.

Picton contains two extensive carriage and waggon factories. Fralick & Brother, on the corner of King and Elizabeth Streets, was established in 1855. In this factory eight hands are employed. Carriages, waggons, sleighs, cutters, &c., are turned out each year to the value of eight thousand dollars.

That of Samuel Hart, on Main Street, was established in 1840, and is now carried on by Hart & Son. They do a very extensive business; twelve hands are kept in constant employ. Carriages, waggons, sleighs, cutters, &c., to the value of twelve thousand dollars, are annually turned out.

There are also two other carriage shops, one of which is conducted by John Thomas, and the other by John Dennison, both on Main Street.

In the manufacture of furniture, chairs and bedsteads, Abram Southard does a good business; his factory is on Main Street; he employs six hands, and turns out articles to the value of four thousand dollars per annum.

R. S. & J. N. Gilbert manufacture furniture, chairs and bedsteads, and give employment to four hands. Rufus Sawyer also manufactures furniture, chairs and bedsteads, and gives employment to four hands.

In Sash, Doors, and Blinds, Planing, &c., the only factory is on Bridge Street.

Prince Edward Tannery is situated on Mary Street, and was established in 1840, and is owned by Mrs. Hubbs, and carried on by John Carrington. It employs eight hands, and turns out about eight thousand dollars worth per annum.

That of John Mallett, on Ferguson Street, employs eight hands, and turns out 30,000 sheep skins, 2,000 cow hides, and 5,000 calf skins annually.

Picton contains one Brewery; it has been established for many years, and is carried on by Charles Pickering, situate on Water Street.

FLAX MILLS.

NEWSPAPERS AND PERIODICALS.

" The Picton *Times*,"—Established in 1854. Published every Tuesday by Robert Boyle, at $1.00 per annum. Office, Main Street, (opposite Wesleyan Methodist Church.)

" The Picton *Gazette*,"—Published every Friday, by Conger & Brother, at $2.00 per annum. Office, Main Street, (opposite the store of C. Gearing.)

" The *North American*,"—Published every Thursday, by McMullen & Brother, at $1.50 per annum. Office, opposite the Post Offic.

STEAMBOATS.

Steamer " Bay of Quinte," F. A. Carroll, Master. Plies daily between Kingston and Belleville, arriving at 8 P.M., for Belleville. Returning, arrives at 9 A.M. for Kingston.

Steamer "St. Helen," E. Smith, Master, Plies weekly between Montreal and Trenton, arriving at 12 M. Saturday. Returning, arrives at 12 M. Monday.

BOARD OF HEALTH.

R. A. Norman.

EXPRESS OFFICE.

John A. Rawson, Agent. Office in the Post Office, Main Street.

TELEGRAPH OFFICE.

John A. Rawson, Agent and Operator, Main Street.

ISSUER OF MARRIAGE LICENSES.

David Barker, Esquire, Main Street.

CUSTOM HOUSE.

Office. Main Street; John P. Roblin, Collector; John S. Clute, Clerk.

BANK OF MONTREAL, PICTON BRANCH.

Main Street; James Gray Agent; Fred. White, Accountant.

INLAND REVENUE INSPECTOR.

Charles Smith, Revenue Inspector : Office, Main Street.

C. HAIGHT & CO.,

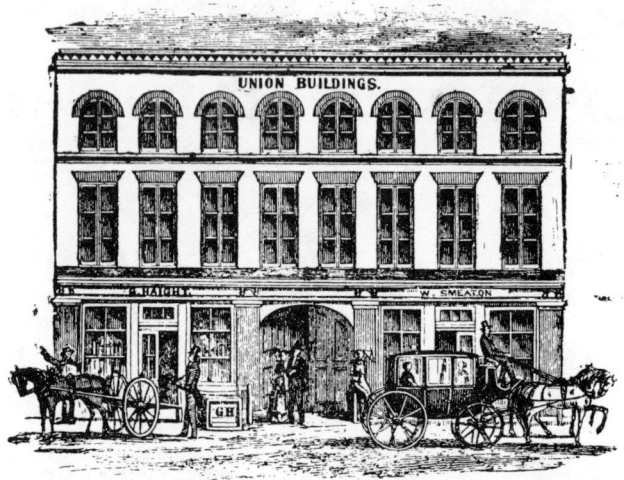

CHEMISTS AND DRUGGISTS,

AND DEALERS IN

Paints, Oils, Dye-Stuffs, Window Glass,

BRUSHES, LAMPS,

School and Miscellaneous Books,

STATIONERY,

FANCY GOODS, ROOM PAPERS,

GARDEN AND FIELD SEEDS.

We import our PAINTS, PAINT OILS, Garden Seeds, and Room Papers.

Our Stock is large and well selected. We spare no pains to buy low, which enables us to **SELL CHEAP.** Call and see.

Union Buildings, MAIN STREET,

PICTON, C. W.

THE GAZETTE,

A CONSERVATIVE JOURNAL,

Established Dec. 20, 1830,

— IS —

PUBLISHED EVERY FRIDAY MORNING,

Nearly opposite the Bank of Montreal, **PICTON,**

And contains all that goes to make up a First-class Country Newspaper.

A MAMMOTH

Subscribe for the best !

Subscribe for the Gazette !

POWER PRESS

Has recently been added to the GAZETTE OFFICE, which enables the Proprietors to print a paper which must give satisfaction.

TO ADVERTISERS.

The GAZETTE circulates in every neighbourhood in the County of Prince Edward, besides it has a large circulation outside, and is consequently a good medium through which the public can be reached. Our terms are so low that all can afford to advertise, and none can afford to neglect so important a source of profit. Call and learn our prices.

THE BOOK AND JOB DEPARTMENT

Is very complete, and we are now doing better work, at a cheaper rate, than can be done in this or adjoining Counties. Printing in Gold or Colors neatly and cheaply executed. We only ask a trial!

DEEDS, MORTGAGES, and OTHER BLANKS, always on hand, or printed to order, at a cheap rate. Enquire our prices before going elsewhere.

CONGER & BRO.

PHILIP LOW,

PICTON,

Crown Attorney

AND

CLERK OF THE PEACE,

Solicitor in Chancery,

AND

NOTARY PUBLIC.

105

FRIENDS' SEMINARY,

NEAR PICTON, C. W.

HAVING leased this well-known Institution, we now inform the public that it is open for the admission of Pupils of both sexes.

THE WINTER TERM

will commence during the Eleventh Month (November,) of each year, and continue twenty-two weeks, followed by a vacation of two weeks.

THE SUMMER TERM

will commence during the Fifth Month (May,) of each year, and continue twenty-two weeks.

It is the design of the Institution to afford a safe and pleasant retreat for the children of Friends and others, where parents may, with confidence, place them. Care will be taken of the health, and also to promote good moral habits in the Students. All unecessary visiting on the First day of the week is strongly advised against.

Pupils are required to furnish their own Soap and Towels, and all articles of Clothing must be conspicuously marked, with the owner's name in full.

No Scholar will be admitted for less than half a term, nor unless sustaining a good moral character.

TERMS:

For Board, Washing, and Tuition, $50 per term, payable one-half at commencement, and the remainder at the midle of the term. No deduction will be made for absence for less than half a term, expect in case of sickness.

☞Applications should be made early.

All communications must be post-paid, and addressed to M. O. NICHOLS, Picton, C. W.

MOSES O. NICHOLS,
ALICE S. NICHOLS.

N.B.—The Seminary is situated in the Township of Hollowell, County Prince Edward, on the Picton and Bloomfield Road, two and a-half miles from the former place, in a section of country which, for beautiful scenery and healthiness of location, is unsurpassed in America.

GREAT WESTERN
Railway,

OF CANADA,

FROM

SUSPENSION BRIDGE, Niagara Falls, TO DETROIT,

229 MILES.

BRANCHES,—From HAMILTON to TORONTO, 39 Miles; From HARRISBURG to GUELPH, 27 Miles; and from KOMOKA to SARNIA, 51 Miles. Total, 246 Miles.

OFFICERS.

THOMAS SWINYARD........	GENERAL MANAGER.
THOMAS BELL...............	TREASURER.
JAMES CHARLTON..........	GENERAL AGENT.
W. WALLACE...................	PASSENGER SUPERINTENDENT.
W. ORR............................	FREIGHT SUP'T EASTERN DIVISION.
J. PEACOCK	FREIGHT SUP'T WESTERN DIVISION.
G. L. REID......................	CHIEF ENGINEER.
S. SHARP........................	MECHANICAL SUPERINTENDENT.
Æ. IRVING, Q. C..............	SOLICITOR.

CURRY & REYNOLDS,

DEALERS IN

Fancy and Staple Dry Goods,

~~GROCERIES, AND BOOTS AND SHOES,~~

MAIN STREET, PICTON.

G. C. CURRY. W. P. REYNOLDS.

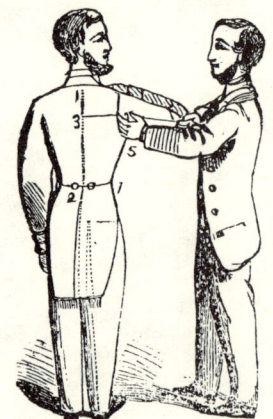

W. T. YARWOOD,

Merchant Tailor,

DEALER IN

READY-MADE CLOTHING

— AND —

Gentlemen's Furnishing Goods.

Mr. JAS. DUNLAP, (late of Boston,) Cutter.

All orders executed with neatness and despatch.

Main Street, PICTON.

FRALICK & BRO.,

MANUFACTURERS OF

CARRIAGES AND SLEIGHS,

OF ALL DESCRIPTIONS,

Cor. of King and Elizabeth Sts., PICTON.

As the work done in this establishment is so well known (having repeatedly taken first prizes at the Provincial and County Shows,) it is needless to say more than that we are at all times prepared to turn out work second to none in Canada.
BENT STUFF for Carriages and Sleighs of all kinds manufactured on the premises.
Picton, Dec., 1865. **FRALICK & BRO.**

A Portfolio
of Prince Edward County
Aerial Photographs
by Lloyd E. Thompson

Lloyd E. Thompson is well-known in Canada for his portraits of celebrities, dignitaries and statesmen.

In recent years Mr. Thompson has broadened his horizons to industrial illustration in which he has become quite successful.

The accompanying portfolio of aerial photographs illustrate some communities of Prince Edward County.

Mr. Thompson lives in Northport and has his studio in Picton.

Picton and harbour.

Skyway Bridge over Bay of Quinte.

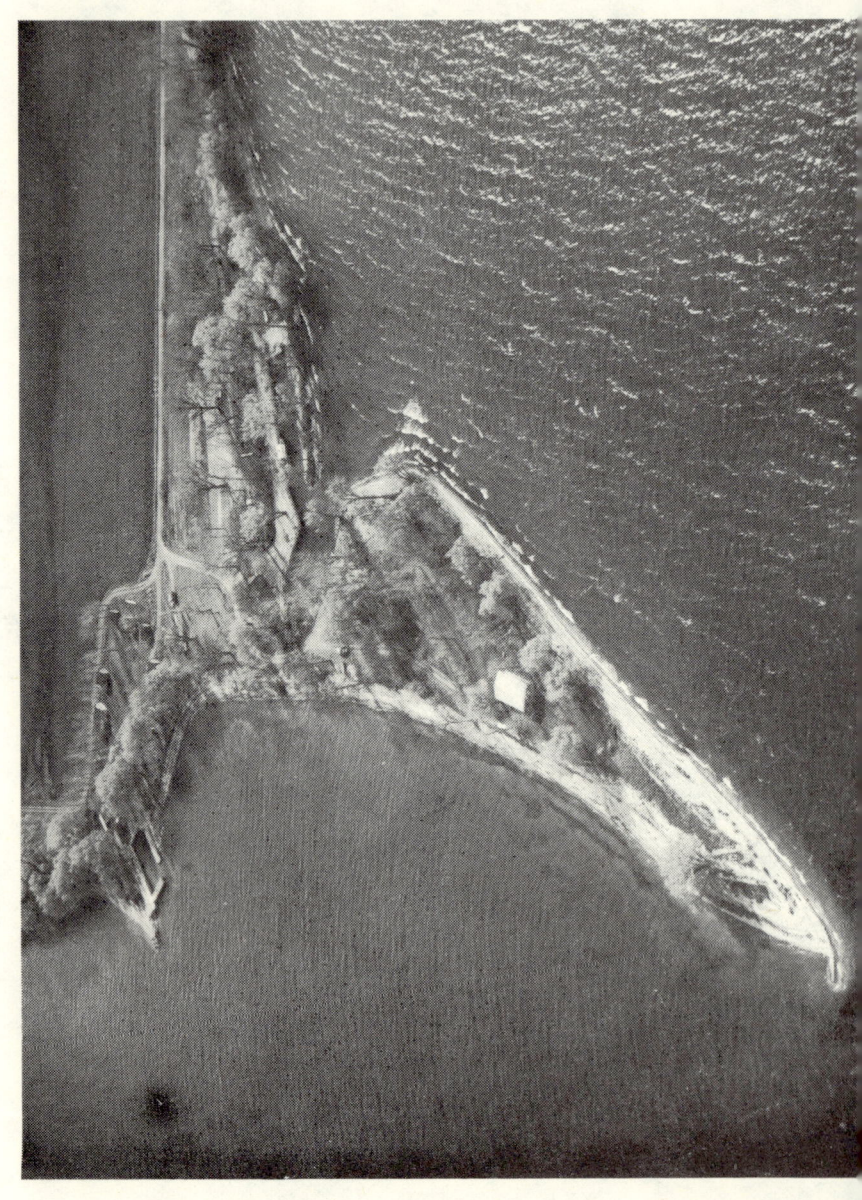

Prinyer's Cove, Cressy.

Black Creek Bridge and Cheese Factory.

Scotch Bonnet lighthouse. Nicholson's Island.

Salmon Point lighthouse.

Point Traverse Cove.

West entrance Murray Canal from Brighton Bay.

Marin Donahe Island, on the west coast, being inhospitable land, was used

Main Duck lighthouse.

Glenora ferries during winter service.

Lake-on-the-Mountain and Glenora.

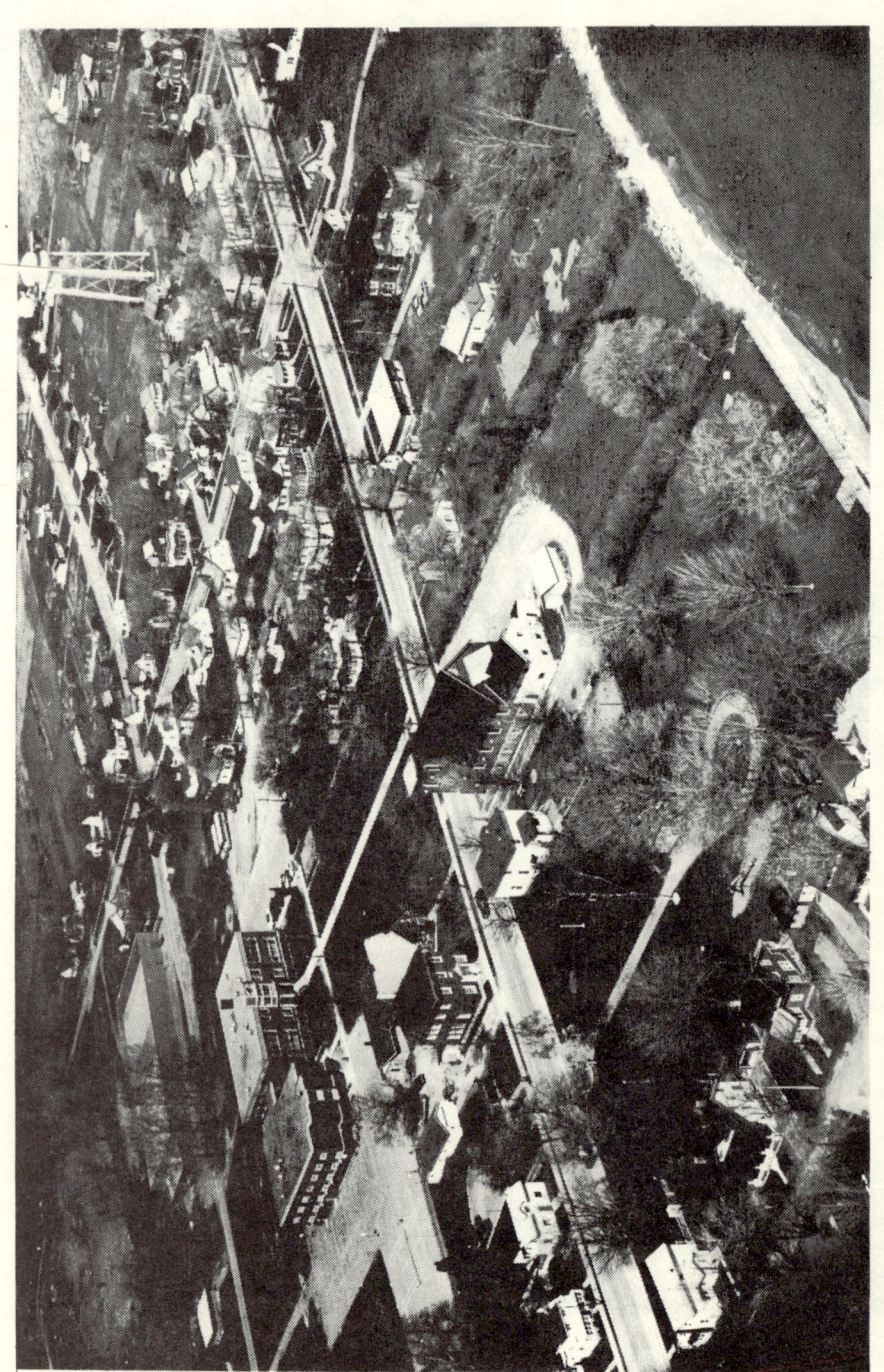

SBN 0-920028-00-4